# Serial Consciousness

# Serial Consciousness

## Greg Branson

The Eye of Gaza Press

# Serial Consciousness

This edition was first published in Great Britain 2011

Copyright © 2010 Greg Branson

Edited by Carol Costa

Cover mandala © Sarah Charlton

Graphics by Matt Ryalls & Alan Hancock

IBSN number 978-1-873545-06-5

The right of Greg Branson to be identified as the author of this work has been asserted by him in accordance with the Copyright, Designs and Patents Act, 1988. No portion of this book may be reproduced or utilised in any form or by any means, electronic, mechanical, including photocopying or retrieval system, without the prior permission in writing of the publisher. Nor is it to be circulated in any form or binding or cover other than in which it is presented.

All rights reserved.

Published by the Eye of Gaza Press,
45c St Augustine's Rd, London NW1 9RL
(0207 713 7159)

Printed in the UK by CPI William Clowes Beccles NR34 7TL

# Contents

| | | |
|---|---|---|
| Chapter 1 | The Creative Purpose | 1 |
| Chapter 2 | Descent to Earth | 11 |
| Chapter 3 | Human Evolution | 20 |
| Chapter 4 | Reincarnation Defined | 34 |
| Chapter 5 | Serial Consciousness | 53 |
| Chapter 6 | The Next Life | 72 |
| Chapter 7 | When Life Begins | 93 |
| Chapter 8 | Karma Explored | 111 |
| Chapter 9 | Soul Qualities | 120 |
| Chapter 10 | Intricate Planning | 135 |
| Chapter 11 | Resolving the Issues | 155 |
| Chapter 12 | Global Karma | 172 |
| Chapter 13 | The Quickening | 186 |
| Chapter 14 | Future Plans | 203 |

# GREG BRANSON & HIS MISSION

Some of the more effective spiritual teachers are the ones who choose to beaver away quietly out of the public eye within the particular communities they serve. They are content to spend many years building up a vital spiritual initiative, part of a nationwide network that will, at the right moment, lift the country up onto a higher arc of being. Greg Branson is one such person.

This is a time of great change, and many light centres are needed to support the emergence of a new order from out of the present turbulence in world affairs. For these people to be in the public domain too early, before the foundations of their work are complete, and before they have developed sufficient spiritual resilience, is risky. And the population needs to be ready to receive their new understanding. There is no point otherwise.

Greg is a true visionary, someone able to delve into the higher worlds and inner Earth with exceptional clarity. He has used his abilities to organise a team of Earth energy workers on a 30 year mission to discover and awaken many important power centres and chakra points around Britain and, particularly, to reinforce the London energy grid. It is exacting work to strengthen and protect these sites from misuse, and awaken them when the time is right. There are few people willing to take this kind of challenge on.

Another of Greg's tasks is to empower organisations that have strayed off their path. He is rarely thanked for his efforts. Greg sees himself as a spiritual trouble-shooter and his work requires him to release past energies that are blocking the present. This takes him around England, and regularly to sites in the United States and Australia held tight in the intractable energies that belong to an earlier age and have outworn their usefulness.

He is also an accomplished healer who has developed more powerful ways to focus the mind, harnessing and directing the subtle energies with such precision that people with severe physical or emotional conditions can be brought into harmony by effectively arousing their own natural healing ability.

Greg's understanding of past lives is second to none and his approach to past-life therapy is unique. He realised early on that the usual ways of looking at this subject were either limited or misguided. Every person is different and there is usually a complex pattern of past lives that requires a very flexible and sensitive handling, if they are to be relieved of their karmic burden.

This book is a definitive work. There are few aspects of the subject that have not been comprehensively covered. It is the result of a lifetime's investigation and experience, and Greg feels that it is now time for his understanding and methods to be brought to a wider audience. However, his ideas are rarely comfortable for people determined to believe what they have always believed. Truth is many layered and spiritual seekers uncover each layer only when they are ready. Greg's thorough approach will help his readers to achieve this.

# 1
# The Creative Purpose

As humanity awakens to a new global consciousness it is increasingly important that higher spiritual knowledge, for so long the province of esoteric groups, is now made available to all who wish to consider it. Though the ideas on reincarnation contained in this book may provide a much expanded view, they are by no means the absolute.

Earth abounds with fanciful notions. Those who see spiritual seeking as glamourous and exciting, enthusiastically respond to beliefs and practices that give them an inflated view of themselves and their pathway; yet, these are merely some of the trifles that so easily trap the unwary. They choose to indulge in wishful thinking, and this is not confined to individuals. It can be found, most significantly, with those Western religions that are content to advocate beliefs that deny what so many in the Eastern countries know to be so. Yet, even in the Oriental and Indian belief structures, understanding is limited, and spiritual truth is often misunderstood in quite a different way.

Many eminent thinkers look on life as a haphazard, accidental progression. You just happen to be in this body, at this time, through an absolutely arbitrary series of events that brought you into being. A random sperm fertilised the egg; talents and intelligence came with the genetic package. Darwinian theory asserts that human evolution happens only by natural selection, and refutes any suggestion that there could possibly be a Divine presence involved in the process.

There are two main views of God from the Christian perspective. The Deist approach asserts that 'He' created the universe, imbued it with an evolutionary momentum, granted humanity the necessary gift of free will, and then let us get on with it.

## The Creative Purpose

The alternative Theist belief says that 'He' still plays a direct, personal, hands-on role in daily affairs. This view is fundamentally flawed if you believe that God is 'All there is', because then 'He' cannot be merely one of the players in an expanding and, therefore, incomplete, universe.

Whether one believes that God directs and motivates each life personally, or merely provides the Source matter needed to initiate and sustain a personal journey in this world, the creationists are certain that there is a Divine evolutionary impulse that overrides mere chance, bringing to the scheme of things what is currently referred to as 'intelligent design'. However, scientists are quite able to keep these faith-based beliefs at bay with the demand, "Prove it!"

There are so many questions to ponder that can never be completely answered. Scientists today know much more about what makes up this universe and even how it came into being, yet still not "Why?" and certainly not "From where?" The conundrum, "If God created the universe, then who created God?" that stops Christian thinkers in their tracks, remains unanswered and unanswerable. This mind-numbing exercise is wasted effort, for God, the Absolute, has no cause. "How can this be?" one might ask, but this enquiry comes from a mindset limited to cause and effect, matter and anti-matter. And so, the reply would have to be, "Only God knows." It all returns to faith in the end.

Faith, however, has to be a flexible thing, capable of being re-interpreted as new waves of understanding come in. Both sides must acknowledge their limitations. There are always those who refuse to believe the evidence, however convincing, for reasons that are born not of scepticism but of blind certainty. Science has estimated the time of the 'big bang', and can date many events throughout the vast span of history, yet many fundamental Christians push this evidence aside to fit their own conceptions.

A few individual scientists are true visionaries. They know instinctively that there is no more comprehensive self-deception than to believe that the physical dimension is all there is, that there is no penetration by the supernatural realms which, in any case, does not guarantee the existence of an absolute creator. It can be argued that heaven exists, and God does not.

Christians must avoid opposing the godless Darwinians. Taking sides prevents the deeper nuances of truth arising. The only point in locking horns with the atheists' contrary position, is to draw your adversaries out and, in uncovering the inconsistencies in their arguments, you can, through reflection, know something of your own.

Many religious people in this country accept the evidence of history rather than the Old Testament myths. They accept DNA but, "Of course, God must be behind that, too". Scientists talk about the 'big bang' without a whisper as to a possible cause, yet by breaking down the limitations of current conceptual orthodoxy they are venturing into some of the realms that are traditionally the province of mysticism.

No one within the creation can ever know or isolate the Creator and, indeed, in realms not so far above this one, there is no separation in the way we can understand it.

Science has the upper hand today. It can point to an incredible flush of discovery over the past century. The atom has been split, space has been breached and planets explored, while medical science has helped doctors treat the illnesses that took so many young lives in past ages. Science is the achiever. But, even though scientific progress continues to be revered and relied on, a role it has wrested from the churches, it is totally unable to provide any spiritual sustenance or guidance, particularly when our political leaders continue to kowtow to the multi-nationals that exploit scientific discovery, passing laws and promoting agendas that are bordering on the insane.

**Questioning the status quo**
Many courageous folk, with legitimate doubts about the way humanity is heading, are striving to uncover those ever shifting layers of shared self-deception which, when challenged, will inevitably draw on the seductive or belligerent shadow forces to severely test the resolve of these worthy people.

The end of the Piscean era has seen an escalating dissolution of the certainties, as nature and fate fight back against the kind of moral blindness that always occurs when the shadow is either ignored or projected onto others.

Many Christian leaders have become too tentative or distracted to speak out strongly on the really big moral issues of our day, let alone try to explore and expand their core supernatural beliefs and teachings. These need to be brought out of the realm of superstition into a coherent and acceptable form that will truly satisfy a questioning mind not caught up in the ritual and dogma. There is a crisis of faith, and it is the relatively minor issues that are threatening to shatter the integrity of their communion.

The Catholic Church has been particularly slow to redefine and so, re-invigorate its reason for existence, acknowledging that the world of spirit interpenetrates with this world and that the power to heal and to perform miracles remains alive in their midst. This is part of the Christian heritage, and Jesus, who incarnated humbly, would not wish that anyone be denied the gifts he demonstrated so effectively during his time on Earth.

For so long, the Church of Rome has defensively proclaimed that only priests should heal or communicate with higher beings, that saints must be miracle workers, and popes are infallible. This exclusivist approach leaves ordinary churchgoers, who feel the stirrings of a long suppressed hunger for personal spiritual revelation, wondering where they belong.

Those who experienced flashes of psychic activity, or who had a wish to be instruments of healing, gravitated to the Spiritualist movement, which was necessarily brought into being through inspiration from the higher realms to plug the gap left by the hidebound attitudes of the orthodox churches. There was a pressing need to bring forward some of the new teachings and the psychic gifts that confirm life after death and establish the relevance of the heavenly worlds to the here and now. Still, in recent times, many Spiritualist churches have retreated into their own version of cosy superiority, where the young and the discerning feel out of place. It is no wonder that many people are turning to bizarre alternatives.

In the commercial spiritual arena, there are the 'prosperity consciousness' seminars, 'speaking to angels' workshops, and the like, which hoodwink people into believing that it is possible to bypass the hard grind of spiritual discipline in order to get something for nothing. Speak to any top sports person or opera singer, and ask if they would have reached such heights without hours of practice and attention to detail. Yet, so many people view spiritual practice as not requiring that kind of dedication. For them, a blessing from 'On High' has been granted merely because they believe in their own divinity. It will require a great deal of soul-searching for this kind of person to achieve even a modicum of true and lasting release from the heaviness and restriction of Earth existence. Without this honesty, progress is likely to be delayed until life, in some way, forces them to confront their inner deceivers.

Today, an increasing number of people, loosely defining themselves as Christian, are questioning certain dogmatic teachings of their faith, such as: "Did Jesus, destined to be overshadowed by the Christ while remaining very much a human being, really have a virgin birth, when that event would have made him superhuman?" Then there is Hell, that terrifying place resurrected as stark images from many a childhood contact with the shadow worlds. Would a compassionate God create a place of perpetual damnation for unrepentant sinners? It is unlikely.

Nevertheless, as in the past, it is the celestial realms that can lure 'lost sheep' back into the fold. The possibility of angels watching over humankind remains fascinating to even the most sceptical person, but the far off Christian heaven, restricted to the especially virtuous, is no longer the trump card it was in those scientifically unenlightened eras. The afterlife must be viewed as a here and now reality that can be contacted directly in ways appropriate to these faster and more sophisticated times.

If a loving God has granted free will to all His Earth children, why do many of the churches and faiths demand total allegiance to mere interpretations of truth handed down unchanged over thousands of years? Why do their leaders decry and vilify as heretics those who question the detail of religious doctrine? How can they bring themselves to stone a young woman to death, as still happens today in some parts of the world, when their authority is challenged? These are issues that urgently need to be addressed.

**Further soul progression**
Darwinian theorists see each new life as the irrepressible product of natural selection within an entirely self-determined universe; all people, whether part of a persistent thrust towards greater perfection or not, have an arbitary amount of brain power and artistic potential, and so on. Thus, giants of the past such as Shakespeare, Buddha, Einstein, and Jesus came about entirely by chance.

Traditional Christians, on the other hand, would see them as having been miraculously granted higher abilities by God, to be examples to the unenlightened masses struggling below; certainly not as a fortuitous convergence of existing genetic components. Yet, they are not so removed from Darwinian theory when they say that each human being is born without the accumulation of personal experience and expertise carefully pieced together over many millennia.

If the Master Jesus had had no prior experience through many Earth bodies from which to draw the inspiration and spiritual stamina for his very challenging mission, then it would have been like plucking a primitive man from the Amazon jungle and electing him president of the United States. The leap in human evolution would have been far too great.

Christian orthodoxy wants us to believe that each unique human life is a gift from the Creator that can take any form that He wishes; thus, DNA is marshalled in its Divine specificity for a higher purpose, and nothing precedes it. This, of course, begs the question: Would the omniscient One really want to take the time to create billions of humans exactly as they emerge at the beginning of a life, denying them free will from the outset, when each new soul could just as easily take up a precise position within the evolutionary flow of the Christ consciousness working through human evolution, and marshal itself into a clearly defined progression, without such Divine intervention.

I believe that your progress as a spiritual being can never be over-ruled by a 'higher authority' without your permission, even if standing up for your truth leads to your own personal Calvary. A closer look at some of the interpretations of the great teachings will reveal the ways that orthodoxy presents fables as fact. And this is evident, no more starkly so, than when men of self-proclaimed importance, often claiming Divine inspiration, have used the ideas contained in the Book of Revelation as a justification for actions that were severely motivated and harshly executed.

**Divinity aroused**
Over the past few years, an increasing number of people have felt an enlivening impulse arise from deep within, which they sense comes from a higher source. They instinctively know that they must shy clear of the dictatorial pronouncements of many who represent the orthodox paths and those who trumpet some of the more contentious New Age beliefs. For spirituality, in the coming times, must arise solely from personal attunement. Certainly, experiences will continue to be shared, but the greater understanding that rises from the unconscious depths must now be the prime arbiter of what is spiritual truth for each individual, and this, the great mystics, prophets and visionaries have always known.

While the Christian heaven remains a closed door and ecclesiastical thinking a closed shop, individuals must contact the inner worlds and truths for themselves, in whatever way is appropriate for them. Truth always seems more complex than people are ready to absorb. Yet, in reality, it is far simpler, for in any moment there is only one idea to embrace and one step to be taken.

It is true that development achieved on higher planes is occasionally held back, and then, as has been seen in recent times, allowed to surge through into physical reality as a very big evolutionary leap forward without any apparent reason. While Earth, at its highest, is totally attuned to the great evolutionary cycles, its ability to bring through the awakened consciousness that accompanies them, is dependent on the maturity of all life forms on the planet, not only the human.

## The Creative Purpose

To understand how humankind has achieved such rapid intellectual progress over the past one hundred years, without a commensurate ability to handle the moral challenges that came with it, it is necessary to look much further than natural selection or Divine intervention.

What comes through to meet the increased sophistication of opportunity, so often contains distorted energies inherited from a far past that corrupt the natural wish for self-advancement. Life will always challenge our status quo, for only then can the set beliefs and restraining influences be dislodged, revealing the many possibilities set out for this life and beyond.

I believe that everything that is incomplete when a person moves beyond the physical experience remains embedded in the subtle layers of the Earth until a soul descends to retrieve it, every unsatisfied hope, every unfulfiled ability—which brings me to the main point of this treatise, the need for further human experience to clarify, develop and extend various strands of your individual spiritual development.

This necessitates further forays into the dense world of matter to complete any unfinished business and to enhance the individual creative abilities that have been introduced but not fully explored. A journey was begun long ago, and it is being continued on the physical plane by most of us, following a procedure generally known as reincarnation.

It is time to revisit the esoteric processes common to all great spiritual paths, and this includes becoming more sensitive to the presence of past personalities in the background of our lives as part of the unifying process now required for planetary elevation.

### Further lives

It started out as a very simple flow of experience that an elementary soul entered into in more primitive times—a 'soul' being the inner identity that oversees this present life. It accompanied you to this world and it will be there when you pass on. However, it is much more complicated now as layer upon layer of life experiences have accumulated, leaving a large number of unresolved issues from the past that have been woven into the current destiny pattern, all waiting to be released, all intending to assert their influence as the opportunity arises.

Not everything comes forward at once, however. Some aspects, not relevant to the current phase of this incarnation, remain out of reach, held in the depths of the unconscious until one has sufficient maturity to address them. For instance, a person may have a natural creative gift when young, which probably had gone through a long period of gestation over many lifetimes to establish its full range and potency but, even so, it may still need a prolonged period of development in this life before it can be expressed and sustained in a world that is not always responsive to innovation. The amount of inspiration that can come through is determined by the person's ability to assimilate new ideas and processes.

There is so much to understand on this vast subject of one life following on from another to fully grasp the sheer complex brilliance of our cycles of incarnation, and the inner and outer patterns to which each subscribes. The heaviness of the Earth experience prevents the kind of freedom enjoyed in the worlds beyond, though there are no shortcuts to spiritual maturity even there. For, if the soul restrictions you take with you when you die remain unrecognised and unreleased, they will eventually prevent you from progressing satisfactorily in that realm. It may need another Earth incarnation to rectify this.

This three dimensional existence of ours conforms to laws of simple cause and effect, and most people relate to it mainly through the physical senses. If you could suddenly register, not just another reality as mystics and spiritualist mediums do, but many of them simultaneously, all adhering to different laws, it would be impossible to cope. So, until sufficient spiritual growth has been attained, all experience is necessarily confined to this realm.

Without a spiritual dimension to their lives, many people believe that they are beholden to no one but themselves and this leads to the ego building up a false sense of importance. This is the great issue facing many spiritually-minded people today, for as their understanding, ability, and influence increases, the need for true humility increases also. No one, faced with the need to relinquish personal power of any kind, does so easily, that is, until the recognition comes from the deep places within the heart, that all power resides with the Creator.

We are all making a journey through worlds and dominions, inspired by the belief that we are gods in the making, that we are amassing spiritual expertise, and that one day we will be like Jesus. It can be quite a jolt to realise that we are treading a totally personal Earth journey, over vast tracts of time, in order to discover a magnificence that can only be experienced in the moment that is upon us; and as we embrace the opportunities revealed by the higher ones, this richness is magnified each time a new soul descends to Earth.

Life is not a punishment for barely remembered sins, as it so often seems, nor a redemptive treadmill. Rather, it is a perfect opportunity, in the perpetual search for personal fulfilment, to consign all desire to the scrap heap of eternity. Then joy will take over, it certainly will, as each new ray of light is directed through the diamond of truth into various nooks and crannies of your chosen destiny pattern and far beyond.

# 2
# Descent to Earth

God's creation is a vast complex of worlds and dimensions each with its own unique set of precise laws and procedures. It is true that these interpenetrate, but a move from one to the other requires a body that can adapt effectively to the conditions found there. When you consider that the fields experienced by individuals on most other planets are outside the range of what we can register as physical, any explanation of the intricacies of this creation having multiple realms must inevitably be restricted in human understanding.

We are all rightly confined to the human experience, limited to easily understood experiences that connect up. Imagine being linked to one hundred radio channels simultaneously bombarding your attention and you will understand why there are veils to memory that prevent many earlier experiences of this life intruding on your present circumstances. These filters enable us to have some sense of proportion, spared what we are not yet required to know, and what it is no longer necessary to remember, so that the essentials of each day are achievable and can be integrated into the fabric of just one life at a time.

"Living in the now", as the popular term goes, requires a mechanism that allows one to do this. A conscious mind is needed that can relate to this moment, with a subconscious aspect to bring forward, from all sources of personal experience, exactly what the moment is requiring. And you can't do without an ego—your identity in human terms—to facilitate your journey on this planet, even though it rarely understands what its true role is.

Although today, more and more people are attuning to rays that touch the infinite, and are receiving flashes of understanding that can begin to bring diverse strands and fields of experience into a unified focus, there are few people around to help them to achieve this without a painful struggle.

This book is an attempt to lift commonly held ideas into a heightened comprehension accessible to many people. The past can then breathe more effectively into the future and the future into the past, and the light can descend to Earth through us and, with the dark element rising to meet it, we can open out to more subtle truths about ourselves and those we relate to. And, by harnessing the collective intensity of this, we can help the planet lift itself up onto a higher rung of achievement.

**Lord of the Universe**
At the beginning, the single, all encompassing Source Mind was comprised of two complementary expressions of consciousness that had no sense of being separate, the simple inauguration of what would become a complex interaction of duality, where the nuances of light and dark would play out their destiny.

In order to develop the various sub-divisions and areas within the full scope of the Godhead, it was necessary to receive sparks of expansive energy from the Ultimate, exploratory swirls of love and aliveness, that had the effect of uncoupling the two components of this Unified Presence which could continue to blend in harmony, but did not have to. It was by granting free will as a non-retractable gift to this dual-natured existence, that creative diversity is able to flourish within it.

A most important thing to know is that one of the two aspects of this, now divided, Presence is orientated to the origin of all light, while at the same time allowing it to shine creatively wherever it can reach, to all available parts of itself unconditionally; while, simultaneously, the other aspect traces the thought pulses to the limits, yet here the dark is equally not isolated, it needs to allow all of its vast experience to be returned to the Source.

Absolute light within the solar system is at a single point at the centre of the Sun, and absolute dark is at the extremities, with eternal light forever making love to eternal night. Yet, there is nowhere that light is not, and nowhere that dark is not. They are compelled to work together always. However, imbalance is inevitable, for without the need for re-unification, no creative activy could happen at all.

If you stand in the doorway of a well-lit room on a cloudy moonless night and face the darkness, the darkness is what you will see. On the other hand, if you stand in the doorway, with your back to the darkness and face the light, the light is all you will see. You believe what you perceive. This demonstrates that the dark and the light are two aspects of the same dynamic that is 'you'. But, when you cease blocking the way, you will be aware that the light is forever transforming the dark and the dark is forever transforming the light.

The great Creative Mind was never fooled into believing that either aspect should have precedence over the other, except in the sense that when you breathe in, an out-breath is required to complete the cycle. It is vital that neither the dark nor the light is ever denied or used as a weapon by the ego, for polarisation always holds back progress. They are both natural and essential.

In the beginning, there was no form in existence as we would understand it, just thought; and while the creative rhythm continued to be sustained, the balance between the expansion of the full scope of darkness and the automatic return of all experience to the light, left the one great Dual Mind in complete harmony. But it could not last, for as the new creative sparks were used for the expansion of the give and take of thought within the creation, it became clear that the two that existed within the one would have to be extended to include the many.

Some people call these two components of consciousness, the involutionary and the evolutionary. The reach of the dark, the involutionary, is the slowest vibrational rate achieved at all points at the furthest distance from the Source of Light, and these points increase in number as the process continues. So what does 'evolutionary' actually mean? Which aspect is playing which role?

We like to think that we are evolving, lifting ourselves up beyond past ignorance and overcoming the lower impulses that would drag us down and return us to our former bestial nature. We see the involutionary as the enemy holding us back. But is not the darkness evolving along with the light?

In fact, our Sun is growing gradually weaker as it burns itself out, and the universe is expanding and creating more darkness, and that is how the unified 'God' wishes it to be. For this is one of the great paradoxes. The essence of light sacrifices itself to the darkness in order that those entities, including you and me, that lie within its compass, having infinite potential, can continue to achieve that potential. You see, because it all started with that first inbreath towards the light at your birth, and the outbreath towards the dark followed it, the pull of evolution will definitely keep you ahead of the game, but only just.

The dark and the light are everywhere inside of you and all around you, too. Every cell of your body is both dark and light, in almost equal proportions. They come and go in whatever way and to whichever degree you allow them to—for these two Divine aspects will not normally invade you, they will not override your free will. But if you try to have one without the other, watch out. Any continuing imbalance between the dark and the light, or between the two within the one, I define as karma.

So, as the great Dual Mind grew in complexity, the constant need for re-unification became more and more cumbersome, and this required the breaking up of its function into twelve sub-minds each with their light and dark aspects. As, for example, if you and your partner start a business and gradually take on more staff, a time will come when you will need to create departments or subsidiaries, even as the two of you remain the owners and in charge.

## The Evolutionary Plan

I must stress that much of the detail from this point on, the exact figures, for example, are only given so that you can understand the general principles involved. There are always exceptions and other systems co-existing.

The whole structure of evolution on these higher planes is of a quite different order from anything that a human mind could contemplate, particularly now that the universe has matured. But it is possible to gain a sense of the way it actually works if the explanation of the planes, including the levels within them and their inter-relationship, is kept as simple and precisely structured as it was near the beginning. It is only necessary to have a general idea of how it all fits together as a natural and expanding process of creative interaction between the light and the dark.

The basic concept, integral to all future explanations, is that, for individual consciousness to descend from a subtle to a less compact realm, a source entity must identify a set of linked concentrations of creative intent, functioning as individual minds within it, and project these down, in turn, to a denser, slower level of itself.

So, in order to accommodate an expanding potential, and develop it into more active formations, the One Entity, with the highest intensity of light at its centre and the darkest realm at its periphery, separated the two primary parts of itself into twelve unique sub-divisions of beneficial intention, twelve heart beats, which were divided, not into compartments as you might imagine, but into concentrations of creative energy which then intermingled. These became the guiding creative principles which would manifest individually as twelve minds on a denser level, each having one-twelfth of their core vibrational potency, and able to explore that newly created realm in an apparently separate manner.

The plane that these twelve occupied was eventually divided into seven layers of energy, each requiring a hierachy of sub-minds to take on the responsibility for directing the many diverse streams of intention coming from the Source Mind into integrated forms of creative expression within it.

Once the seven main levels of the first plane were completed, the expansion of the Primary Consciousness moved into a new phase with a complete change of emphasis and reversed polarities. The twelve and their sub-divisions split up into twelve further parts that individually extended the divine purpose into denser regions of itself, each requiring a twelfth of the power. Thus, a second plane was brought into being with all its layers being occupied by many sub-minds that would initiate and motivate the activities appropriate to the scope and specific needs of that expanded realm.

Each of these minds took up an intimate marshalling brief to facilitate the creative expression of the many impulses and directives from the first plane, drawing this into a cohesive whole. It must be mentioned that every subdivision, and the subdivisions of those, are infinite in their potential.

From that initial 'stepping down' of the One Mind into a denser part of itself, while at the same time occupying it—for there is nothing other than itself—it formulated a series of intricate thought constructions of such immense potency that they manifested progressively as sustainable expressions of itself on all the planes below, right down through the physical plane, which is the sixth, to the seventh which I view as the 'plane of becoming'. Each of the planes progressively enjoyed a much more defined sense of order and tangible purpose. It must be stressed that the polarity of each successive level is reversed in order that the sub-minds established within them will experience a kind of autonomy.

Everything that exists in the physical universe was brought into being and sustained by a complex, evolving thought process within higher consciousness that was projected down through the levels of itself. So, from a level of the first plane, a set of twelve powerful expressions of divine purpose, projected intense concentrations of creative thought sequentially into each of the planes, eventually finding physical expression as all the solar systems of this galaxy.

**The Essential Sun**
On a high level of each plane, the twelve differentiated energies oversee a realm that is layered into seven levels of frequency which function rather like the octaves of the musical scale. On a subtle level of the third plane, there is the creative dynamo that lies behind what was to manifest eventually as the physical Sun which, in its turn, initiated and supported the twelve mighty concentrations of evolutionary intention that lie behind the major planets in this solar system.

Each of these exhibits its own unique archetypal nature, in much the same way that the twelve signs of the zodiac have their own particular characteristics but, nevertheless, remain still very much integrated into the whole.

It is necessary here to look at the way in which the Sun actually exists overall, for the Sun you see in the sky is actually only the core of the spiritual Sun. That statement will probably require some thought. Putting it another way, the multi-levelled Sun is the whole solar system. And all other single suns embrace their particular solar systems in the same way.

So, though this cannot be registered with human eyes, everything within the solar system, without exception, is part of the Sun. Therefore, you are a small part of the mind that is the Sun, and as the physical Earth is part of the Sun, you are a small part of the Earth, too.

You will be more aware of being positioned within the Sun when operating in a higher consciousness, for there you will experience no focus of light—light just is, to the degree that you can stand its intensity, and the dark just is, to the extent that you can endure its vast brooding silence. The rays of light are everywhere, inside and out, and always matched by a complementary expression of the dark energy. In the world of matter, separation is the biggest illusion of all.

**Archetypal Consciousness**
The vast concerns of creation are formulated on the first plane and passed on to the twelve planetary Lords, positioned on the perimeter of the core of the spiritual Sun. The most important of these, from the human perspective, is the Christ consciousness which allows a creative purpose down into a vast array of archetypal minds beneath it on lower levels of the second plane.

These include the 'Genesis' energy, that initiates and develops many global concepts and sends concentrations of creative thought into expressions of itself on the third plane, the lesser archetypes, which can mobilise human endeavour in more precise ways. These are the national archetypes, the racial archetypes, and the religious archetypes. On the next rung down, there are the minds behind the various art forms, the minds that develop structures of governance, and those behind a host of other types of collective human activity such as the professions. However, they would not even contemplate incarnating directly into a human body; the intensity of the power would blow it apart.

It is not just human evolution that the Christ energy supports; it also assists the Lords of Planetary Evolution based on the third plane which have been given names such as Mikaal and Raphael. On their own level these angelic beings have no such personal identity.

Then, from the cusp of the third plane, the Christ energy supports the animal kingdoms, the plant kingdoms, the kingdoms within the seas, and the various elemental forms of evolution, the 'fairy folk', who, from the beginning, were concerned with conditioning the atmosphere around the fiery orb that was Earth, and one advanced team of elemental workers was entrusted with the task of establishing and maintaining gravity, so precisely, that lasting divisions of consciousness could sustain their evolution within its influence.

These elementals are linked to the great archetypal mind that created and continues to integrate the four elements, fire, water, air and earth, which bring about precise form and function on all the lower planes. Currently, these are seriously skewed towards 'fire' which has caused so much destruction on the planet in recent times and will continue to do so for quite awhile, in conjunction with 'water' that has seen emotionalism run riot in the age of Pisces.

Certainly, the air element of heightened communication that marks the Age of Aquarius is becoming more accentuated today, but many souls, still passionately orientated towards the Piscean ways of control, are continuing to resist it, and the beleaguered Earth is bearing the brunt. Consequently, the natural and necessary phase of 'global warming' has been over stimulated and dangerously exaggerated.

### The Power of Two
It is here that the concept of duality must be expanded. The one became the two, and these were to follow their complementary

paths of exploration and consolidation. The masculine principle was precisely orientated within the unified source of light and, from that position, it sought to further the reach of the dark, an expansive dynamic that has enabled the various planes supporting individual experience to be progressively established, with the whole forever venturing into the unknown. The feminine principle has its home at the vast frontiers of creation, but needs to lift the fruits of experience by all manifested beings up to the light. This was expressed simply by our forebears when they blessed and celebrated the crops in their harvest festivals.

The evolutionary process is humanity's prime focus but, of course, without a growing universe there can be no further individualised forms possible and no advancement for those that already exist. So, the dark and the light need each other in order to manifest a balanced creative principle into form within all solar systems, all galaxies and, indeed, into all planes of existence, now and in subsequent expressions of now.

Yet, despite the separation of the core creative element into two distinct dynamics, they continue to exist within each other, and the more evolved a form of creation is, the more completely it can experience this blending. At this time, when the two ages are merging, the Piscean and the Aquarian, there is a determination by the shadow forces to prevent them coming together in the kind of unified relationship that is needed. It is vital that we achieve much greater harmony at this time before the dual influence behind planetary affairs once again swings away from a precise balance, taking the planet gradually towards a quite different kind of polarisation.

The Master Jesus came to Earth, soon after the Arien age had passed into the Piscean, to set into place profound new ways of approaching unity; but after one thousand years, the ability to register and implement the dominant principle, unconditionl love, had retreated, and during those 'dark ages', the evolving human consciousness was at its least enlightened. However, to balance this, consciousness on the level above was at its most heightened. So, you see, in the extremes of duality, nothing is ever as it appears to be.

# 3
# Human Evolution

All life forms on the planet are a small part of the Christ consciousness, not separate from it, as many religions would have us believe. From its elevated position on the second plane, a subdivision of the Christ energy sends 'evolutionary waves' into denser forms of itself. The various solar ages could be likened to breaths of Christ consciousness, progressively extending individuality into intelligently conceived, increasingly diverse forms throughout its entire domain.

There have been many of these 'breaths' over the history of this planet that have supported the large collective initiatives, known as 'group souls'. As they expanded in influence, these concentrations of consciousness have sub-divided and settled on lower levels of the second plane as 'spirit families'. When in their usual pattern, these 'families' are a collection of one thousand individual minds, with six interlocked families making up each composite group entity.

A 'family member' is an individual consciousness within the energy of the collective. So, the human you is a division of your own personal source energy, or archetypal self, that has been projected down through each of the levels of your being into human form, where you are probably relating closely to other members of your spirit family throughout this incarnation.

It is more likely that your partner is from one of the 'cousin' groups than from your own immediate family, because karma is easily created in close relationships, and every family wants a minimum of negative karma between its members built up over time, particularly the kind that tends to grow in intensity the more the participants are exposed to it. So, Plato was in one family, Aristotle in another, and Socrates in another still. Related, certainly, but not intimately so.

Each 'group soul' is a sphere of conscious energy that surrounds the Earth on a subtle level, and extends its influence down to include all the spirit families orientated within it on lower vibrational levels of the second plane. Your source mind is precisely situated on the level of the third plane appropriate to your degree of evolution in a form that psychics see as a body of light, but it also has a dark aspect. I would prefer to call it a 'body of pure presence'. Each separate human consciousness remains entirely within the compass of a spirit family which is likewise securely held within its group consciousness.

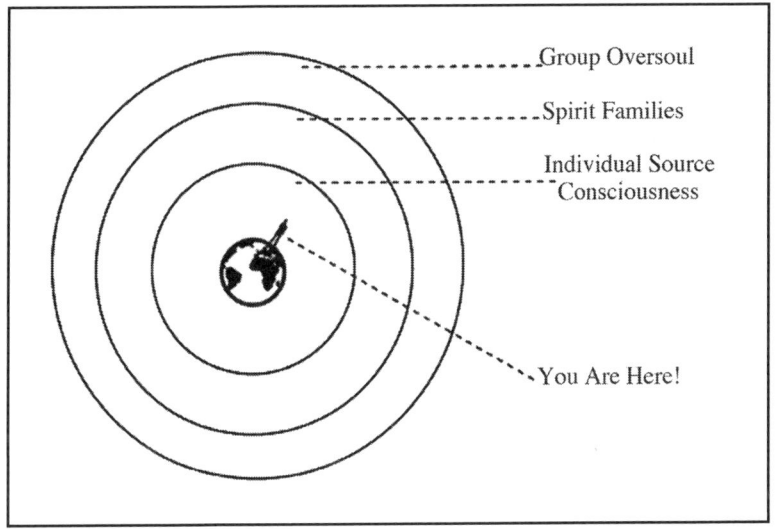

## The Spirit and the Soul

For a life to be established on Earth, two intermediate minds are required to reach from the individual source mind on the third plane to the human being on the sixth; I refer to these as the spirit and the soul. These two vital concentrations of mind are divided and extended to provide sub-minds that enable individuality to be fixed within the succession of bodies that you occupy, the causal body on the third plane, the mental body on the fourth, the astral body on the fifth, with a closely connected combination of two bodies, the etheric and physical, on the sixth plane. And don't forget that all of these have their dark and light aspects.

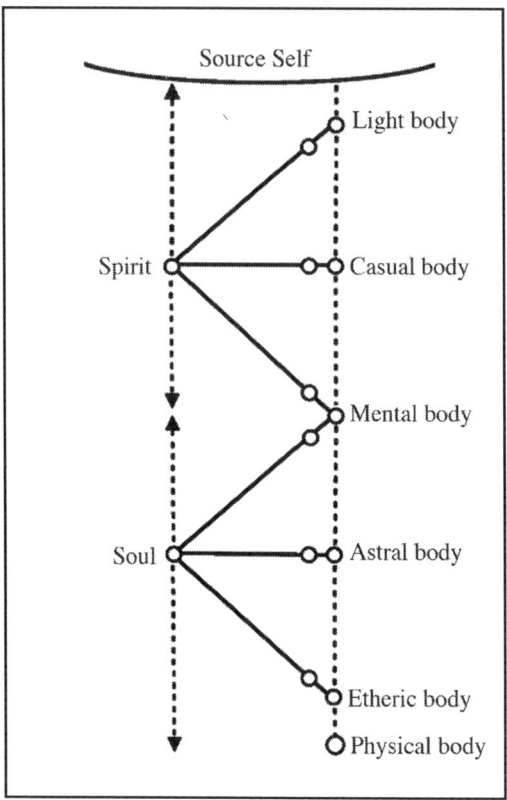

The spirit extends from the source self, down to the evolutionary aspect of the mental body, while the soul balances this by ranging its influence from the involutionary aspect of the mental body right down to the physical you.

As you read this, your full complement of bodies and their attendant minds are both lifted up and held down, which allows your source mind to direct streams of evolutionary consciousness through all of them, when not resisted. Free will is granted even to the individual cells in your body.

In a sense, every created entity is a universe unto itself. This solar system has outer limits as does your physical body, and the planetary system is rather akin to the organs within your body that keep it alive and functioning, with the Sun being the brain and the Earth being the heart.

Extending this analogy, the Christ consciousness on the second plane is divided into various segments, each one projecting purpose into a different compartment of the solar brain. And you are like one cell in the heart of this vast creation wondering how you fit into the whole. You know that you are part of something much greater than yourself and, inevitably, you see the brain as God; though, of course, everything is.

These are complicated notions, that your dual self is spiritual only to the extent that you restrain your human nature, that the outside is to be found inside, and that the human you both exists entirely and does not exist at all as a separate entity.

**Your Whole Existence**
Every level of 'you' includes a mind fragment with a conscious and sub-conscious component that lives through an attached body. But that raises the question, "Where are these bodies?" Spatially, they all lie within the same shape, rather like those Russian Dolls, with each inner form vibrating at the faster frequency appropriate to the plane it occupies.

When you walk around, all your bodies accompany you in a tight formation, with only a limited ability to range beyond your field. The etheric body of psychically active people can easily move a little away from the physical body, though this can be dangerous without strict discipline and training. This is why some people, when under anaesthetics on an operating table, rise above and view what is happening.

The spirit, which psychics see as a tiny orb of light, normally stays within the bodily form; though if there is a severe rejection of the spiritual element in a person, it can be forced outside of it.

However, once there, it becomes very vulnerable to the clutches of a predatory shadow band of spirits.

The pituitary gland has the closest affinity to the presence of spirit. Your soul is also orb-shaped when viewed from a human perspective, and normally resides in the vicinity of the pineal gland. Imagine a ball that has a solid outer shell, yet the next layer within it is vibrating at a faster rate, and the next layer is faster still, and so on. The ball occupies a specific physical space, but is not internally limited by it. Meditate on this because it explains how your spirit and your soul, in conjunction with each other, can span the entire range of your satellite minds and their bodies.

An eternal moment separates the various aspects of your being, enabling you to extend participation to the far reaches of your inner space on every level, in an immediate and personal way. These extremes of frequency exert a profound influence on your physical form. And, needless to say, both the spirit and the soul have light and dark aspects on each of the levels they extend to, these needing to remain integrated and in harmony.

## The Soul Collective

Your individual source consciousness which dispatched the spirit and soul in tandem, can monitor progress and assimilate all experience by alternately focusing deep within them, but there may be different degrees of clarity, rather like when the wave bands in your radio set attract interference.

There are resonances within the soul, as it expands and contracts and expands again, that reflect back to the various stages of the journey from the initial thought within the Ultimate Mind and forward to the perfected Self it will become.

After drawing the consequences of all experience back into its integrated self, as and when this becomes appropriate, and especially at the end of the Earth life, the enhanced qualities and the overall understanding attained will certainly enable the individual source self and, indeed, the universe, to continue to grow in stature.

The active sub-conscious mind on each level is usually not aware of its counterparts but, provided that the soul and the spirit act in unison, they will stimulate a creative purpose and direction into the causal life, the mental life, the astral life and the human life; and then sensitively align all aspects of the complex structure of minds and bodies to the greater purpose that they share. No part, it must be remembered, is more or less important than any other. It is a chain that needs strength in every one of its links.

It is not possible to go backwards spiritually, but it is possible to embed heavy karmic restrictions into the soul. These imbalances and disharmonies, carried over from the physical experience, will make further progress difficult. It only takes the mental process on one level to go out of sync and the whole is impeded.

The etheric body is strongly influenced by its astral counterpart, and must learn to operate through the physical processes in order that many habitual physical functions can flow smoothly, such as breathing and driving a car. In times of crisis, heroic acts are often carried out without recourse to conscious thought. In fact, thought and planning very often get in the way of the etheric flow.

The etheric streams directed into any creative endeavour will lift it beyond what is possible through the human apparatus alone. Where appropriate, the etheric consciousness makes use of the psychic senses to forge a bridge between the human mind and the entities that live on the astral plane.

The various levels of individual expression are actually a layered representation of higher thought that has to be gradually and meticulously revealed. And then the maturing consciousness is able to progressively expand away from the Godhead, to explore the extent of time and space, and towards it, also, with greater confidence.

Each of the exactly positioned set of bodies resonates precisely to the extremities of the plane it occupies but, beyond that, a reversed polarity is encountered in both directions; so it takes flexibility and openness for each resident component of consciousness to overlap its neighbours as paradox is always present.

The worlds are interdependent, as are the various levels of your own composite reality, and the more you can work in concert with all previous expressions of your divine purpose, individually and collectively, and with the other streams of evolution such as the plant and animal kingdoms, the more of a complete expression of divine love you will be. The physical world develops incrementally, and you are part of this natural process, not superior to it.

Also, while you believe that you are standing still on a very stable Earth you are entirely ignoring the greater reality. In actual fact, you are travelling vast distances as the planet revolves around the Sun. You are an intrepid space traveller, experiencing constantly changing cosmic influences. Your astrological relationship with other planets is more important to your destiny flow than you realise, and this significantly affects all of your bodies.

**Astral Consciousness**

Although you cannot see this with the naked eye, the physical bodies of spiritually mature people are vibrating at a faster frequency than less evolved mortals. Here on Earth, spiritual masters can relate directly with those having their first Earth incarnation, but this is rarely possible on any other plane.

On the level above this, astral life has a much narrower focus than our own. On passing, we will be surrounded only by those who share our spiritual and creative interests or, indeed, our base instincts and desires if that is the choice made. Anything immediately above our present level of awareness will be invisible until we lift our eyes and hearts up to it. We may not be aware that beings more evolved than ourselves even exist.

It is far from true that the 'heavenly world' is much easier place to comprehend and live in. The astral consciousness is certainly lighter and more vibrant, but it is no easier to grow spiritually there than in a dense material existence. People can still be trapped in restrictive mindsets for long periods. Higher frequencies can only be tuned into initially using power borrowed from a more evolved spirit. Until you have the ability to relate to these more subtle realities and have begun a process of linking in, they will remain completely beyond the range of your astral senses.

Each level has its limitations to understanding, and distortions of perception that will keep you from making progress before your soul is ready. However, if you work at it, you can gain an inner sight of the various objectives that your spirit family wishes you to achieve, visualisations of the future, if you like, just as you build up mental images of how you would like your present life to unfold. These designs are encountered on all of the various levels of consciousness occupied by you. On the third plane there is a wide range of powerful thought formations that have been built up to support the many common purposes that you might choose to participate in on Earth, such as the religions.

In the ancient Greek culture, the spiritual leaders of that time, and those with creative genius, were on a higher level than many of their contemporaries but, nevertheless, there were a number of group souls in action with many families, across a wide range of spiritual attainment, playing their part within it. That is not to say that a man born rich was more spiritually elevated than a family slave, although that tended to be the case.

The Christ energy influences every group soul directly but, normally, such high energy is only available to us indirectly through an intermediary on the third plane, such as the Master Jesus and those near to his calibre, or from less elevated archetypal energies, also originating on the second plane, that inspired the great Masters, such as the 'heretic' pharaoh Akhenaten, the Buddha, Abraham, Confucius, and many others.

It is important to clearly differentiate between the archetypal energy and the man or woman it was channelled through. The Master Jesus is still overshadowed by the Christ presence and he operates now in his causal body, projecting thoughts down to where they are needed. Soon he will be establishing and working through an etheric orientation to assist those on Earth who have accepted the very exacting task of bringing humanity and the planet through the unsettling challenges that lie ahead.

Some people are expecting Jesus to return in physical form, but he has already served in that way. He will now be available as an inspiration to those wishing to lift themselves into a more ethereal reality, which is becoming possible for many people as the Aquarian age becomes fully operational.

## Exploring contrasts

It is not unusual for a spirit family to divide, with the two parts incarnating under the influence of apparently contrary archetypes such as Christians and Moslems, Catholics and Protestants and, in the last world war, Germans and Jews. This involves very valuable lessons in maintaining harmony when faced by polarised forces.

On the fifth plane there are the smaller shared impulses that lie behind the various extended 'families' on Earth, that form a village community, an isolated tribe or a small ethnic grouping, which reach out into wider contexts only when that is applicable to their evolutionary needs. Within larger cities, these small units intermingle with many other such concentrations of identity and purpose, and must co-exist harmoniously with them.

Do note that the following range of frequency levels are subdivisions for convenience and should not be compared with those put forward in any other teaching. In fact, when you relate to the planes from your Earthly perspective you would call the physical plane, the second, and so on, up the scale to the seventh plane. I have chosen to see it as working downwards from the first cause.

## Your Destiny Path

Both your physical and etheric bodies have an innate intelligence that relates to the surrounding environment through the set of senses each has available, but there is an inner connection that enables them to jointly progress your current life. The etheric energies can come through into the physical and take control in a variety of ways, especially when there is a psychic sensitivity in operation which acts as a bridge between the two minds.

Remember that all of these bodies and minds were planned under direction from your source self before you started your 'descent'. Free will determines how closely they will conform to the etheric destiny patterns when precisely directed streams of intention are channelled through them into your physical reality. Your genetic limitations determine the nature of your brain function and they restrict the extent that your latent aptitudes can be expressed through it. The body can only be changed to a limited extent, with face lifts and sex change operations and heart transplants being some of the experiments. If you should lose a leg in an accident, the etheric leg remains intact.

| **The Expanding Universe** |
|---|
| 1st Plane<br>    Universal Consciousness<br>    The Ultimate Reality<br>    The Father/Mother God<br>    Perfection that cannot be contained |
| 2nd Plane<br>    Christ Consciousness<br>    Archetypal energies<br>    Group Souls<br>    Spirit Families |
| 3rd Plane<br>    The Causal Plane<br>    Planetary Consciousness<br>    The Guidance that supports families & communities<br>    Individual Source Consciousness |
| 4th Plane<br>    The Mental Plane<br>    The Plane where you can understand balance |
| 5th Plane<br>    The Astral Plane<br>    A Place of transition and emotion |
| 6th Plane<br>    The Etheric and Physical levels<br>    The Realm of delayed cause and effect |
| 7th Plane<br>    The Plane of Becoming |

However, your evolutionary intentions, expressed through your destiny pattern, need to be very flexible, leaving scope for a wide range of opportunities to fulfil the requirements set out before you were born. There may be a number of available paths to each major event. For example, from the possible marriage partners available at the outset, the one that will actually come forward is determined by how all of them have progressed by then.

Sometimes, the physical body can no longer be used as a vehicle for a particular part of the outworking; for instance, where a promising athlete is unexpectedly confined to a wheelchair and the destiny pattern has to be modified or some parts of it abandoned altogether. Most close relationships, however, can be continued.

So, while human consciousness responds to precise planetary influences, it has considerable flexibility in its order and timing. The etheric, however, is confined to its basic nature and its commitment to support the physical experience. Nevertheless, while you can evolve by many different routes, trying to force your spiritual development onto higher levels will always attract adverse consequences. Your spiritual stature can only be progressed one step at a time by whatever route you take, and it is a gross delusion to think you can suddenly become a completely transcended being without having prepared for this.

Even before incarnating, some people decide to take on more than they were advised to attempt. "I can do it," they think. "I am strong enough". However, when they descend into the harsh reality of the physical life, they discover it is beyond them. If this over-reaching is severe, the life can become rather chaotic, and when the full force of their unreadiness makes itself felt, some decide that they cannot cope and end their life prematurely.

Fortunately, it is possible for your astral consciousness to delete one of these excess areas which is then neutralised in the soul, and a less complex path replaces it. But stubbornness often sees some of these people battling on with the heavy load, and they get bogged down in the fierce energy resistances they've created.

There are some people, unhappy with such a fleeting lifespan, who pursue the secret of eternal life; they want to continue in this body forever. In future generations, the ageing process will be slower, and people will enjoy fruitful lives for much longer than is possible today. The age of 125 will be easily attainable without too much physical decline. But these 'eternal life' advocates do not understand why it is necessary to die. They do not accept reincarnation and, therefore, do not see that a separate body will be needed to express quite a different range of abilities in the future. Short fingers may not be appropriate for a concert pianist or short legs for a long-distance runner, so they must change to a more appropriate form in a later incarnation.

Many men do not understand or value women because they have rarely chosen to have this experience and lack empathy. Evolution through balance is the main objective of life on this planet and very severe tensions arise when this goes out of kilter and the tendency towards extreme polarisation takes over.

**An Introduction to Evil**
Even though light and dark are the two essential components of all creation, the 'dark' so often appears to be the undesirable element, the one apparently standing in the way of evolution. It is marginalised and repressed, it is ridiculed and, all too often, demonised, and wars are fought to keep it at bay.

They need to work together, these two great creative forces and their sub-divisions, alternately relinquishing control so that the light may extend its influence to the full extent of human achievement and beyond. This is similar to what is happening at the extremities of the solar system. The stillness breathes out there and the elements stream into oblivion. Yet the power to create returns renewed.

The light relinquishes control, surrenders its authority, and so, enhances the understanding and evolution of the countless individual life forms within its scope. The dark and the light are both achievers in their own way. Both retain their glory. Humanity has tried to put a wedge between them for far too long.

Gravity is maintained and extended when the pull towards and the pull away are in an almost exact balance. This precise relationship allows the physical universe to exist, maintain stability, and play host to the myriad life forms upon and within it. Deny any component and force is needed to prevent chaos.

Now, this really does put the cat among the pigeons, for everything pertaining to evil in the Christian belief system will have to be re-thought. Does evil actually exist? Oh yes, most definitely. It is the deliberate and persistent working to unbalance the natural order for personal advantage, and where an individual allows this to grow into a wish for absolute power over a group or nation, it becomes evil on a grand scale.

**Collective Blindness**
A second plane archetype lies behind every religion, providing it with its particular identity and mission. But a renegade projection of that archetype, operating from the third plane, can draw self-serving members of the human family together to devise, promulgate, and enforce systems that distort and demean a particular divine purpose as it is projected towards them.

These ones may be inspired by groups of wayward spirits on the fourth plane, the 'shadow bands', who encourage small groups to break away and form sects that, without proper inner guidance, soon go astray and descend into depravity. But more usually these false leaders remain within the large religion, manipulating the worthy ideals into rigid and off-centre interpretations of the original archetypal message to serve their own agendas, and these distortions are carried forward by many power seekers who follow.

The religious fanatic is much in evidence today, and some are engaging in horrifying acts to destroy what they see as the evil ones in their midst, the heretics, the infidels and the blasphemers. By doing this, they are expecting to earn the favour of God. The less extreme ones, to be found in revivalist settings in America also tread a very narrow path, for the considerable layers of guilt and shame, usually stemming from an earlier religious incarnation, are squashing any attempt by adherents to break away from its influence.

But it is in less obvious ways that the unbalanced ego finds expression in people with the power and inclination to undermine the natural order, as they destroy the architectural heritage of a town or the natural surrounding beauty in the name of 'progress', or they undermine an established system for their own ends and, in the process, become part of a downward spiral.

To counteract these influences from the shadow band, it is important not to try to fix any aberration you see around you, or oppose it. It is much better to find a compatible partner or a group which is operating to high archetypal principles and together build up a more worthy approach on a secure base of unconditional love. This may cause the shadow aspect of the archetype to be aroused in those who are still morally suspect. This is the first phase of the training for any group and when it is successfully undertaken, the retrograde forces operating in your local environment are automatically weakened.

The collective evil, that continues to insidiously weave its web around the planet today, is influencing so many people and diverting them from their true purpose. The aberrant leaders draw many who are weak and misguided into their web of control. These young souls, needing support and guidance from mature influences, become unwitting pawns in an evil perpetrated by groups of debased spirits who have turned completely away from the light.

In the last analysis, motive is everything. And at the time of judgement, which is, in fact, when individuals judge themselves, many factors have to be taken into account before the life can be fairly and properly assessed, and redress undertaken. In the case of the 9/11 attack on the Twin Towers and the subsequent bombing of Iraq, the responsibility lies equally on both sides, for action and reaction are part and parcel of the same dynamic.

Because unconditional love is the rational way to address all divisive situations, both sides have an obligation to understand and heal the conflict, and to do this, it is necessary to look more closely at the difference between the dark element, which is a component of harmony, and evil, which most certainly is not.

# 4
# Reincarnation Defined

**Development of the Individual**
Before engaging the subject of reincarnation, I must introduce a more personal view of your descent to Earth as it may actually have been experienced. You will need to relate everything raised here to a long evolutionary journey down through the spheres, bonded closely within the collective energy of the one thousand souls in your spirit family, and to those from the related families within the scope of your overall group.

Though you probably consider yourself to be a unique, self-motivated individual with a personal destiny to fulfil, you can now see that you are actually a fragment, of a fragment, of a fragment of the great Source mind, set into motion by a single thought of such incredible potency that it could sustain your apparently independent existence throughout eternity, in a vast array of realms and principalities each conforming to quite different sets of laws and procedures based on an over-riding principle of duality—the two within the one, the one within the two—a thought that has led to your current multi-levelled, multi-faceted identity.

As a universal seed of the godhead, there at the beginning, you were taken up by one of the twelve great minds overseeing the solar logos, which directed you down into the next plane as a small part of the Christ consciousness, a creative spark still not yet awakened to any kind of experience beyond your immediate confines—one of many seeds, held together as in a pod. But within that seed you were conscious of the gradual movement away from your moment of creation and this was, even then, the cause of much pain.

The 'oversoul', of which you are a part, was making important decisions, even if you barely understood what they meant; and at some point it was decided that you would develop as a collection of individuals expressing yourselves through the human form, rather than proceed within the animal kingdom, or the tree kingdom or any of the other kingdoms already in existence.

## *Homo sapiens* arrives

The early 'cave dwellers' had an oversoul, but no individuality in the way that we have, nothing that could sustain independent life indefinitely on other levels. They always returned to their source self. This was very similar to the progress of the apes from which humankind was to physically evolve, and most other forms of animal life.

The 'higher self' of a cat dynasty may span the whole range of experience, as a lion, tiger, panther, as well as the familiar domestic kitten, as it moves through its incarnation cycle. Certainly, while there is mutual need, animals loved by humans may be granted the power to sustain life in the spirit world for quite a long time before returning to their oversoul. Dolphins, on the other hand, are beginning to individualise in the human manner. Indeed, if you go to a dolphin sanctuary and swim with them, you may be helping them to achieve this transition.

So, in the early days of man, it had become necessary for more advanced spirits to enter into the bodies of some of the 'cave dwellers' to establish a *homo sapiens* stream of evolution, that could sustain its afterlife indefinitely on levels which directly relate to the physical plane.

A leap in consciousness of this magnitude, involving a complete switch of evolutionary direction, would have taken far too long by Darwin's process of 'natural selection', even if it were possible. In fact, it required but a brief transition from an animal-type evolution to a human one. To achieve this dramatic leap, it was necessary to introduce a 3rd plane consciousness which had already supported this evolutionary step in another part of the Universe. This group of source energies had previously sent incarnations onto a planet within the constellation of Sirius. They were chosen because they had the necessary spiritual maturity and experience to carry out this important mission.

These intrepid pioneers needed to go through an exacting preparation before they could receive an inrush of advanced evolutionary energy into their group consciousness from the Christ entity, which was then stepped down into their various bodies on the planes of descent to the physical environment. To establish *homo sapiens* on Earth was a major undertaking, and it was only achieved after a number of aborted attempts, for although higher beings, mainly from the angelic world, were on hand to impart knowledge and give support, it still took immense courage and inventiveness for each of them to venture onto a planet that had marked differences to the one they had known.

So these pioneers set out on the long journey to a place that is now in southern India where they approached some of the more sensitive of the 'cave-dwellers' and attempted to project an evolutionary thrust through them within the sexual act. It wasn't easy, and often, on the first attempt, the host energy rejected the advance.

Yet, once some of the first wave had succeeded, it became easier for others to follow, and in the course of only a couple of generations, a cluster of truly human beings was established on the planet.

This relatively mature family of spirits knew instinctively that they were part of a great leap in consciousness, and that they were separate from each other in a way that the more primitive family members clearly were not. The capabilities of these advanced *homo sapien* individuals were revered but also feared, and so the early pioneers sought each other out and established enclaves at a distance from their more tribal brethren. They banded together to establish what was to be the first expression of the great Lemurian civilisation.

Centuries later, sizeable enclaves were also established in a western part of South America and near Perth in West Australia. Within the triangle linking these, a significant energy was generated for the development of other Lemurian settlements near various major power points forming a grid of energy that anchored humanity and still does today.

## Your Own Evolution

On the level of your personal source self, where time barely exists, the flow of evolution passed gently through you and by you as a matter of course. Eventually, the energies built up there by the achievements of the pioneers impinged on your group consciousness sufficiently to arouse an evolutionary impulse, and there was a sudden expansion that freed everything up. Clearly, the experience of human life on Earth was needed by some of the seeds in your particular 'pod'.

So, the compact nature of your group soul entity opened out to awaken many of the 'families' of spirits that had, until then, lain dormant within it. They would benefit from the achievements of those pioneers and, in time, a few, then the rest, came to realise that they, too, could follow this example and venture beyond their very limited existence.

Though your own spirit and soul still functioned effectively as one composite mind, and you remained held within the tightly knit bounds of your family energy, there had been an adventurous dynamic aroused in you that stirred up the desire to explore realities that you perceived as external to yourself, the evolving forms 'out there', with mental probes that built up an awareness of the kinds of reality that would eventually be directly experienced by you and members of your family.

You were recognising yourself as a developing being, growing in awareness of what was becoming possible, gradually feeling into what you needed to become, and even though you had not, as yet, a separate body to express yourself through, your mind could clearly sense what lay beyond your immediate experience. It was a stimulating time, for you were already part of the evolution of Earth, even though this was a rather detached involvement.

While this expansion of the entire purpose of your being was happening, you could not help but be caught up in the evolutionary momentum, for a glimpse of the pioneer experiences was relayed back to all those that would follow. You continued to reach out with thought probes into the ethers surrounding this planet, eventually touching into the physical world, and as members of your group soul, including some of your own family, began to join the pioneers, you vicariously shared the thrill of these earliest forays into human existence.

Because you were not fully conscious, there was no sense of urgency. It took as long as it needed to. But you dreamed so often of Earth life and eventually all of you in the 'pod' became capable of registering the extensive range of frequencies required. You became aware of some of the great events that were happening as humanity passed through the many thousands of years it was taking to establish human evolution as a secure and widespread development.

As time passed, you registered the base energies that came in when members of your 'family' fell into states of barbarism. You could not truly understand it, because you were still held far away from the physical plane, and had no personal experience to relate it to; but though human existence was further down the line for you, you nevertheless felt a certain responsibility for what was already taking place, as if you had personally experienced it yourself. There is no separation in reality. We started out as one, and our individual destinies remain forever interwoven; and this was still strongly felt by you.

It is the unresolved remnants of the crude behaviour of some of the early ones that lie behind much of the depravity engulfing the planet today, as humanity tries to reach back to rectify the extreme karmic conditions from those Lemurian times that still remain embedded and active in the earth.

So, the seed mind that you essentially were, continued to grow in awareness throughout the ensuing flow of human evolution, slowly forming a purpose and tentatively developing a clearly defined difference to the others within your 'pod', until it was your turn, your time to become manifest. The early exploits of the family had aroused the courage in your source self to launch its own first journey to Earth, and that would involve breaking away from the cohesive family energy to be an individual in a world that you could still only imagine from your remote perspective.

At the highest level of your existence, the formative aspects of your mind interpenetrate, but the division into spirit and soul ensures that an apparent state of separation exists throughout all the lower realms.

And so began the process of 'descent' from your source self, positioned on a high level of the third plane, as a truly individualised projection from it. The composite 'you' had, for so long, anticipated establishing a spiritual body as a satellite of itself, and now this was happening.

In the same way, as a baby, you did not immediately understand the world you had entered into, so the conscious minds within each of the bodies were, at first, very limited in their awareness. In those early phases of growth, help had to come from outside, on all levels, just as it was given to you by your parents.

Each new embryo body emerged, an 'octave' below the previous one, in a form energetically appropriate to its level of existence, awakened by a creative spark, and linked to complementary concentrations of support positioned at the extremities of that plane. There appears to be but a tenuous connection between the bodies; yet, the chain is unbreakable.

To the spiritual body there was added a 'causal body' on a denser level of the third plane, with a dual consciousness projected into it, giving it an apparently independent existance. It required a substantial pause before entering the planes below, because this was the first time and there was still much about the process to understand and assimilate before the next development was possible. During the pauses, the spirit and the soul continued to separate further in preparation for what was to come.

The limited fragment of spirit consciousness active within the causal body was largely unaware when a completely different aspect of the individual consciousness was being established as an embryo body on the mental level. Sub-conscious awareness within this body includes points on the borderlands of that plane, but extends no further, except by linking through the balance between the spirit and the soul into a greater reality. The soul proceeded to bring the next body into being on the astral plane, and then projected down fragments of its energy into a nascent etheric body and the closely linked embryo physical form.

It may be difficult for you to visualise this exceptionally complex set-up involving incremental shifts in vibration, not outer connections. If you sometimes feel that you could reach out and touch the limits of space that is not surprising, because this is a reflection of the reach into your own inner space. There are also a number of direct links from the periphery of your physical body to points on the borders of the physical plane, points that are yours alone.

At the human level, a connection is made at the moment of birth with the highest and lowest frequencies that limit the range of your physical participation, before immediately returning to a balance point within it, that is to be your orientation in space.

So, you incarnated into a later phase of the Lemurian civilisation, perhaps into a menial role within a tight communal situation. But then, it was strange, because it wasn't you living that life on Earth. Oh yes, your source self was definitely participating in some way, but as you were still conscious in the 'pod', it clearly wasn't you.

**Communication with the Soul**

The soul is closely aligned to your personal Earth journey, and the spirit is a subtle reminder of a higher purpose that extends beyond the concerns of just the one life. Your soul 'breathes' in and out, reaching from a deep place to empower the various strands of your destiny blueprint in stages. When each out-breath nears completion, the balances are re-adjusted and new coping mechanisms invented where the ego still intervenes. So, in its own way and its own time, your spirit sends a succession of energy probes down through the levels of itself, never forcing, never over-riding, always encouraging your human nature to rise up to connect with them when it can. This progressively reveals the ability of your source self to participate effectively in its own creation.

The spirit and the soul touch at the inner balance point deep within the space defined by your physical form. Together, they exercise a subtle influence across the whole range of bodies they oversee. They represent the two halves of the journey of exploration that your source self makes into its own vast inner space, reaching out to where you have come from and to where you are heading, in the knowledge that these are one in this moment and always will be.

If you are able to reach into your heart, in that mystical sense, and are consciously seeking to achieve balance there, you could contact the spirit as it draws on the energy of your soul to inspire you, to lift you into higher consciousness.

It is important to understand that the word 'higher' is not referring to that which is above you, above your head, for everything that you are is contained within the same physical space. There are levels of your being with a more subtle resonance, so 'deeper' is a more accurate word.

The spirit will not speak to you in words or concrete ideas, but through a gentle knowing. Direct contact only comes in a moment of true enlightenment when, resonating through all levels, you register the nature of your true self. Your head will tell you that you are nothing but your heart knows that you are everything, and life must flow an exquisite path between the two, the middle way. On achieving this, you truly will have come of age.

There needs to be a synchronicity of evolutionary development maintained on all levels of your being. However, if your human progress goes ahead of your astral, mental or causal achievement, or drops behind, the imbalance needing to be addressed, the precise alignment to be established, remains your responsibility even after you die. It cannot be passed on to others.

Vibrationally, all human consciousness is a long way from home. Though the spirit and soul together provide the support you need, the connection between them strengthens and wanes periodically, so there are invariably times when you will feel cut off from your essence, your true nature, and from those on the inner levels who have accompanied you on your journey since the beginning, your 'guardians', and from those of your family in spirit who love you. You may even feel abandoned by God.

So, you will need to try even harder to still your mind in meditation when that happens, but remember that your soul not only resides within you, it also contains you. The cultivation of this dual perception is vital if you wish to go beyond those feelings of isolation and, if you are willing to recognise life as your greatest ally, an enhanced creative purpose can then slip through, intelligently directing itself along appropriate lines to reveal the detail set out for this life and much more.

## Existing Reincarnation Theories

To fully understand what reincarnation is and how it works, it is first necessary to consider the most common beliefs that have developed around the world, for the acceptance of reincarnation is not just confined, as many think, to several Eastern religions. It has emerged just about everywhere.

Many people in the early Roman Catholic Church had a belief in pre-existence, which was extended by some to a person having had previous lives, but it basically referred to the prior preparation for just one. The early Church fathers had a doctrinal dilemma. Those with mystical leanings accepted pre-existence, but as time passed, they became outnumbered. The majority, who were more focused on building temporal power, decided that the Church could not be built on confusion if the control they wished to exercise over Europe was to be fully achieved. So they used quite dubious tactics to establish that there is but one soul and one life that begins at the time of conception.

They had to explain away the notable exception, their founder, Jesus of Nazareth, and they did this by providing him with a unique dual nature. Not only was he human like everyone else, a simple man of the people, apprenticed as a carpenter, but to establish his divine credentials, he needed to have had a miraculous birth, and later, at the time of his baptism, he was replaced by the great Christ spirit. From my perspective, I am assuming that the Christ energy came through the point of balance between his soul and his spirit and there was an equal collaboration between the higher and the lower elements of his nature that allowed this.

An absolute papal decree, which did not actually come from the pope, effectively sidelined the many priests who believed in pre-incarnation consciousness and it made the belief in reincarnation even more heretical, and so, it gradually disappeared.

Buddhism, on the other hand, does not accept the existence of an individual soul. Buddhists believe that the human condition is a conduit for life to continue. Therefore, as the mental process grows and creates and unfolds moment to moment, by the end of the life there is an accumulation of qualities that have to progress, they cannot just disappear, and so, as in nature, an ending is a new beginning.

In Buddhist philosophy, when we die, our existence at that moment will pass to a child being born shortly after. In some ways it is rather like when a snooker ball hits another. It is not that the content of one life passes to the other, but some direction and momentum are transferred. Others liken it to when milk turns into yoghurt. The milk is longer there, but it was needed for the yoghurt to exist. Clearly these analogies are simplistic.

They believe in continuity but no individual identity flowing from one life to the next, nothing is fixed, everything remains in motion in the eternal now. As only awareness continues, the state of mind at the end of the life is very important. The beliefs held, the moral attitudes, are passed on.

From the Buddhist perspective, everything is vested in a succession of moments of evolutionary existence known as 'life', and because the qualities and intentions, good and ill, are all that carries over, karma is not held to be a personal responsibility. The Christian belief in accountability at the pearly gates of heaven is unacceptable to them. Without a soul to retain the detail and responsibility of karma, everything outside of the present moment must be illusion.

Buddha knew the tendency of the human ego to distort and demean the ways of the spirit, and it is not surprising that his teachings compensate for this. When one sees the manner in which so many Western leaders wilfully misinterpret the biblical teaching "Thou shalt not kill", the Buddhist path of true compassion is, indeed, very compelling.

It is significant that the initial Buddhist teachings were reinforced by those who followed, in rural communities, monasteries and other centres of learning. They could not help but assume that the continuation beyond death would be in similar surroundings, where life was fairly unchanging and moral progress was generated within their established hierarchies of spiritual and communal life.

The Buddhists also believe that you can incarnate next in the body of a bird or an animal, which from my perspective, rarely happens, for each of the streams of evolution develop separately. So, this possibility will not be addressed further.

While Buddhist orthodoxy teaches that most people are unaware of the detail of life leading into life, the high lamas have reached a stage of refinement enabling them to actively engage in the intricate process of transition, known as the 'bardo', which some believe takes place in a timeless moment, and others, over forty-nine days. It is a period between the experience of ultimate nature and the new birth to come. The Dalai Llama believes that his tradition will be passed on to a specific baby boy in this way, and he will then cease to participate any further in consciousness, because there is no 'he' to do this.

My assertion is that, while it may be true that the next in the line of progression that embodies the purpose of the Dalai Llama incarnates soon after, it is likely to be another representative of a group of souls from the same spirit family that have taken responsibility for this country and its religious life, and not the soul of the present holder of that post, which would return to the spirit world in the same manner as everyone else. There is usually no point in doing exactly the same thing, life after life. It would frustrate the spirit and make it extremely unbalanced. I believe that in the next life, it is likely that he will explore some quite different area of experience.

It is worth noting that if instantaneous reincarnation were true, it would be a way of finding common ground with the scientists, for then evolution would remain a process entirely of the physical dimension. But, of course, it is not.

### Does one soul fit all?
Passing now to the most common belief system, found in the Hindu tradition, in parts of Africa, in the Nordic countries, in the beliefs of

the Hassidic Jews, in the 'dreamtime' of the Australian Aborigines, and in most early European traditions, such the Celtic. All of these belief systems share a similar perspective that could be described as the 'Yo-Yo Theory', where one soul is repeatedly projected down into a succession of lives backed by the sum total of all the experience accumulated in this and other realms of involvement.

The soul approaches the material world using a vehicle that is 'programmed' to give solidity to things built up as a result of the experiences it had in its most recent life, and these will encourage their extension into the particular form and purpose of the next. In early incarnations, with few experiences to draw on, the lives are very simply planned; for example, where the main concern in a life as a fisherman in a small coastal village is family. Whatever the outcome, the soul returns to the spirit world where it takes time to recover and assimilate all that has taken place, and only then does the opportunity come for further human experience.

In a response to this, the spirit of the fisherman, which has a relatively clear overview, impulses the purpose for a further incarnation into the soul; and another physical body, reflecting the needs of that dispensation, is prepared. The birth-time is decided, taking into account the precise astrological components, and perhaps a different sexed body is chosen this time, with the life planned for a quite different location, though probably still close to the sea to keep alive that affinity. Other important details are put in place, such as, who the parents are likely to be and the DNA that will determine the basic mental and emotional nature, as well as the physical form and stamina of the body.

Clear and flexible channels need to be established in the subtle levels of the mind for the soul's intentions to flow through, so that when one phase has been completed, another can be activated at the appropriate time.

Although drawing on actual experience, these new plans are completely untested in the harsh rigour of physical experience. It is rather like when you have scaled the Matahorn in one life and, based on the expertise gained, you decide to take on Mount Everest in the next. But perhaps you feel attracted to a somewhat different kind of experience, such as, the study of volcanoes. Although you continue to draw on all your old skills, this new life requires completely new areas of expertise and understanding which can only be fully developed once the life has begun. The training will come from experienced people passing on their skills that you can add to. The discipline undertaken will establish conduits for the evolutionary energies to be focussed through, but only to the degree that they have been developed first in spirit.

The new challenges will require an expanded capability, and this is taken into account when the soul concentrates a dual aspect of itself into the embryonic forms. One of the tasks of the spirit entities who prepare the way is to inject a receptive energy into the etheric body of the egg within the mother that, when intercourse takes place, will act as a magnet to draw exactly the required sperm towards the egg, the one that will be compelled to reach that destination before all the others, lagging behind, that may have many, but not all, of the characteristics needed.

The mother's etheric body will normally encourage the child's etheric form to encourage physical growth according to the required specifications. But, when the desires of the parents interfere, or when genetic engineering is employed to eliminate what are seen as deformities and tendencies towards future illness, the spontaneous abortion of the foetus might be chosen by a soul unsure of its place.

Outside manipulations are usually inappropriate. The body that comes forth is always the one that the incoming soul requires. It is sheer arrogance for parents or doctors to over-ride those decisions, to believe that this soul does not know what it needs for the coming life. If, for some reason, the body will not be as originally intended, due perhaps to the unexpected illness of the mother during pregnancy, a miscarriage is likely. If the pregnancy does proceed, then it is likely that the physical body may remain somewhat at odds with its destiny throughout its life and the etheric counterpart will have to effect some compensation.

Many early Hindu teachers believed that every life is a direct extension of the previous one. Like the ancient Egyptians before them, they interpreted this to mean that a member of the ruling class would incarnate into the same position, and 'untouchables' would remain 'untouchables'—and always in the same sex body. Life would follow life in this rigid manner, gaining more and more expertise but this, of course, would come at the cost of future lives being inflexible and unbalanced. The idea that you could move from one kind of existence to another; that you could, from lifetime to lifetime, jump from being a sailor, to being a prostitute, astronomer, actor, nurse, farmer, and in different communities in other lands, was outside their range of perception. Now, with the breaking down of class barriers, many Hindus recognise that a diversity of experiences will enrich the divine nature.

They have come to accept that, while the whole collection of past experience and expertise is available, not all of it becomes active. Any part of a life may be drawn on as a starting position for the next one; for example, as a child born into a farming community. He has been a farmer before, but this must be held back for, in this life, he needs to be a heart surgeon. His parents may not understand this; it is stretching their traditional comprehension, but nevertheless, it is their duty to encourage it.

Today, the Hindu philosophy acknowledges that one would be overwhelmed by the complexity of this past if it was all expressing itself concurrently, particularly if there is a great deal of karma. It would also prevent the unwavering attention to detail required for this specialised kind of medical work. It would arouse disturbing emotions that undermine the stability and precision needed and so, clearly, certain karmic energies must be put on hold, to be worked on in a later life specifically set aside for them. The Hindu mind is generally very patient, and this notion of gradual spiritual progress is quite acceptable to them.

Here, I must mention a comment often made to me. "The picture I have of the afterlife is of all my friends and loved ones being there to greet me when I pass. But it seems from some theories I have encountered that many of my family and friends will be down on Earth in new bodies, and unavailable".

This conundrum has perplexed many people. Certainly, if true, it would destroy the whole fabric of any group of friends or family that you might wish to be kept intact. In fact, continuity is a vital part of the transition into the astral world. Loved ones are a vital part of this.

There is much to learn and discover in the afterlife, so detaching yourself from the influences and preoccupations of your human experience will be paramount. The 'next life' will be the last thing on your mind. You have a new reality to explore, and none of the spirit advisors will ever try to force you to undertake further experience on Earth. It will always be a matter of free choice.

**The Theosophist teachings**
No study of reincarnation beliefs would be complete without discussing those of the Theosophists, who have quite a sophisticated view of the one-soul theory that includes the various higher bodies introduced earlier. Following death, it is necessary to assimilate any strong feelings and attitudes that have carried over from the recently completed life. The selfish, isolationist human mind constructs very rigid beliefs and wayward thought processes that can hold back progress. Theosophists believe that these must be released before a move into the mental body could even be contemplated. However, once exposed, the very natural, but limiting, human expressions of regret and shame and longing for forgiveness rise up and, if indulged, can hamper the unlocking of new potential. The soul must find a truly liberated expression before it is able to return to the causal body, its natural home, free of these restrictions.

Within the safe confines of the causal body, the soul begins to relate the life's experiences back to the initial intention, so that any discrepancies and distortions can be reconciled. It is then returned to a state of innocence and renewal, before another incarnation is called for, that will enable further development in a physical world that has since moved on. After that, the details of a new life are drawn into a complex anticipation and a new set of bodies is established sequentially that will bring the soul back towards the Earth atmosphere. These Theosophist teachings certainly provide a more complete understanding of the yo-yo theory which does not jar with my viewpoint except, crucially, in their belief that the one soul returns over and over again.

## You live only once
The Christian belief that each soul is unique and does not return is actually not so far off the mark. This is likely to be your last life on Earth regardless of whether you have completed all you came to achieve, or whether you have incurred negative karma or not. You will not be returning, none of us will.

It is true, that you are personally responsible for everything that you have ever thought and done, and you alone can work out the negative karma accumulated during your life. Karma incurred on one level cannot be discharged on another. So, from those statements, it seems that a new life is required to build on earlier experience and there does need to be some kind of continuity of personal involvement in the outworking; and yet, here it is being asserted that you won't be coming back at all. That apparently knocks the theory of reincarnation firmly on its head, doesn't it? So, I need to resolve the contradictions for you.

It is the crux of this teaching that a new soul is established for each incarnation which does not obliterate the earlier ones. When a soul is spoken of as having reincarnated, it implies that it is the same particle of being that is clothed afresh in a new earth body, but I am asserting that this is not what happens—except that there is one fairly rare exception to this. A baby or very small child who is thrown out of incarnation before its time, may have the veil of forgetfulness placed around it and the soul is given a second chance. But, in the main, there is only one earth life possible for each soul.

## The Orange Theory
This viewpoint brings us to a common belief held by some practitioners in this field. Consider an orange. It looks whole, but when you remove the skin you find a number of separate segments beneath, each with several pips inside. Now, you can remove one of the segments, introduce it into the earth conditions, and return it to the orange after the life is over. Later, the next segment is given its

experience in a life that may have no obvious connections to the first. Each of these segments represents a separate personality, with quite different developmental needs, that puts on the appropriate garb of an earthly form. New skills are required to face the new opportunities and more exacting challenges that will accompany this development.

Now, the orange is, in fact, what I call the personal source self or oversoul. The segments are linked manifestations of thought, within an integrated entity that can project down a unique soul consciousness into a human body, before returning 'home' at the end of that life.

This process is repeated again and again until the entire set of segments has had its turn on Earth. Each incarnation in the sequence needs a different collection of evolutionary experiences; one could be as a farmer and a husband learning to be in harmony within a family and with nature; one as a nun and a cook learning to nourish both the soul and the body; another as a scientist who, in his early days as an athlete, learnt physical precision, to encourage the intellectual precision that would be needed later; then there is the one who is both a violinist and a lay preacher, learning to communicate an elevated sensitivity in different ways; and so on. No segment returns into incarnation, and afterwards the individual retains a separate identity within the whole. Karma can be positive or negative, and any carry-over from the experiences of former segments filters through within the collective consciousness to be an influence for a later life, so there can be elements from a range of former lives blending into the present one.

Indeed, at the beginning of a particular life, the new soul lacks experience, but when you look into a baby's eyes you can often see the vast wisdom of the ages shining through. It is coming from the spirit, so closely linked to the source self, but this soon retreats as the baby gradually opens up to the Earth conditions.

Each life starts out backed by a destiny pattern that provides its potential, growing into the many-faceted representation of the segment it needs to become by the end of the life. At the beginning, the segment is made up of subtle and semi-formed consciousness, an embryo in every sense of the word. It then receives a layered set of intentions focussed in from the current needs of the expanding, sublimely creative source self. The later segments, spurred on by the confidence that comes with experience, can start to venture into some of the very dark and heavy places in the universe and, in learning to reach further away from their source without harm coming to them, greater resilience is developed.

Our analogous orange retains a collective integrity and continues to evolve and integrate the fruits of experience drawing on this to provide material to support a more mature human sensibility in each further life as it is taken on. Of course, it can send out other probes, where necessary, into other planes and dimensions, when a particular kind of experience is required. The portion of the orange on Earth will have a strong sense of being a separate consciousness until it eventually learns that while it is not, in fact, the whole, it does have a purpose greater than itself. As at no time does the entire orange visit Earth and none of the segments has more than one life, the expression reincarnation is, therefore, misleading. A much more accurate expression is 'Serial Consciousness'.

Now, you may well be asking yourself, "So, where does the heavenly afterlife come into this if there is a prompt return to the higher self?" Unresolved karma is an anchor to the soul, and can only be worked out on the plane on which it was incurred; it cannot be taken back to the source. So, the 'orange theorists' could suggest that, with the greater sight afforded to it in the spirit world, there is a process of sorting out, of integration and release, of letting go of the attachment to earthly desires, thus separating the 'segment' from its remaining karmic burden. This convoluted energy is left behind and put into long-term storage for a future 'segment' to work on. The process culminates in the act of receiving grace. The karma is not fully worked out but, in this belief structure, it does mean that it will not prevent the soul from returning to its source.

It is almost as if the seeds of karma are planted energetically into the Earth and, in some season to come, they are awakened when the source mind dispatches a different segment, and the karma is automatically drawn up into it.

## Reincarnation Defined

"Ah, but just a moment," you may be thinking, "this still doesn't explain how it is possible for wise souls, who were last on Earth thousands of years ago, to speak through mediums when you have just said that each soul does not stay very long in the heavenly worlds before returning to its source. How are they able to talk to us?" It is because, once again, the 'orange theory' doesn't stand up to close scrutiny.

# 5
# Serial Consciousness

To return to the source has always been a strong urge in the human psyche, whether it is seen as graduating to the Christian heaven or more esoterically; but I was never impressed by the parable of the prodigal son in the bible with its promise of the welcoming arms of a wise and loving heavenly father after a life of wayward adventuring and dashed hopes, and a permanently tranquil and contented after-life to follow.

Imagine that your source self, symbolised by the orange and containing perhaps 200 past life segments, is a large celestial residence and you must remain there for the rest of eternity. You will be stuck with the somewhat authoritarian father that you left to get away from. He's a little more mellow now in his old age and welcomes you home enthusiastically, but after a while you see that he still doesn't really think your view of life is all that great. He likes being in charge, being obeyed; and there is his wife who was a dutiful muddle of frustrated maternal instincts and unfulfiled artistic abilities when on Earth.

You are great pals with a niece whose promising career as an actress was cut short, and you adore the slightly dotty aunt who loves to dance. But there is also that brother you don't get on with, a reclusive philosopher who thinks he is intellectually superior to the rest of you, and the gregarious uncle who loves to tell stories you've heard before, and the cousin who gossips and flirts shamelessly. They are all living with you, and you can't leave home, you can't get away from them, ever.

Now, I am assuming that your soul family is more mature than that, and you are returning to your source self to be with a set of past lives who have achieved much; such as the astronomer who was incarnate at the time of Galileo and can see into the mysteries of the stars with exceptional clarity and the Victorian naturalist who is eager to share his interest in the evolution of flowers, but that's not really your field. And there is the big hearted mother who loves everybody, and the priest who tortured people during the Spanish Inquisition.

Even if he and the others have progressed since in the collection of mutable identities that is the source self, they will still have completely different interests and ambitions. You want to be with people like you, but that's not the way it works there. The ability to blend disparate strands of consciousness is a very mature skill, and there are few on the planet today who possess it to any great extent. You only have to look at how our leaders behave towards each other as an indicator of where humanity has reached collectively. So, in a world decidedly lacking in co-operation, humanity has a lot to learn before true world government is possible, and the lion can lie down with the lamb.

How many friends are you really close to, who share your passions and can accept your rather awkward nature? I certainly don't know how to fit in well with people who are not like me, who don't share at least some of my interests and beliefs. In my younger days, I felt unrecognised and unloved by my Earth father and a society that didn't accept me as I was. I rebelled against their narrowness and indifference and went off to explore many countries where I had loads of fascinating adventures. Looking back, I have no regrets, I accept who I am and value my journey, the freedom it allows me, and I want to keep going.

Possibly, at some point, I might tire of my daily trudge through time and opportunity, with its unending resistance to my insatiable desire to achieve, and the relentless need to keep going against the odds. I may eventually come to accept that there is, indeed, no place like home – but I doubt it. A holiday, yes, a temporary respite in some heaven or safe haven but, as our lives reflect precisely the degree of maturity of our source selves, it is clear to me that a permanent step off the wheel of karma is not a realistic option for any of us, just yet. As I see it, there will inevitably be a very long delay while we laggards catch up, and there may be a need for further Earth lives before we can finally blend into one cohesive whole.

You will remember my earlier mention of the twelve splitting up to allow descent and so, as you are a one-twelfth part, functioning on a level of one twelfth potency, for as long as any of you wish to remain separate from the other eleven, you must all continue to develop on a slower frequency. The soul presence behind each life does not, indeed, cannot ascend further than its attraction to individualised expression will allow, and that is also collectively true. Although the light will be encouraging all of the component souls to return to the source, the pull of the dark element will continue to expand their reach, which leads to greater refinement and elevation for the source self. That is the supreme paradox.

**Further Human Experience**
The more I look at myself, the more things in my nature I see as restrictions to higher achievement, and some of them have hardly shifted at all over the years. I have spent my whole life exploring my individuality in human form and it is likely that working out my remaining defects and deficiencies will require me to continue relating to the Earth in some way.

However, I could never accept the notion that when I reach the other side and want to meet up with my mother, I would be told that she is 'that child down there in India'. It is the way many people view reincarnation without really considering that to enter as a foetus into a new body, in a different age, a different environment, and in a body of the opposite sex, would probably destroy much of their unique identity.

Frankly, the thought of having to be contained in another human body, handing over any of my individuality to a new personality, and be restricted to the inflexible laws of this physical condition, over and over again, with no power to act independently, when there is a vast universe out there to explore, appals me.

Fortunately, it doesn't happen that way. We are exactly where we are in the evolutionary flow, and I am certain that we can exercise our individual free will, always. Surely, you will want to remain entirely as yourself when you die, and not be absorbed into a collective super-conscious state, any more than you would wish to hand over your individual identity to the quite different reality of a subsequent life on Earth.

As your human self represents the aspect of consciousness most distant from your source, it is likely that your conscious mind will shed its physical and etheric bodies and move on into the astral afterlife as everyone else does, remaining there until you have attained the required spiritual capability to rise to your rightful position on one of the higher mental levels, but no further. There you will continue to forge your unique path, free and unfettered, adapting the interests and skills that you honed on Earth to the purely mental forms of expression appropriate to your new environment.

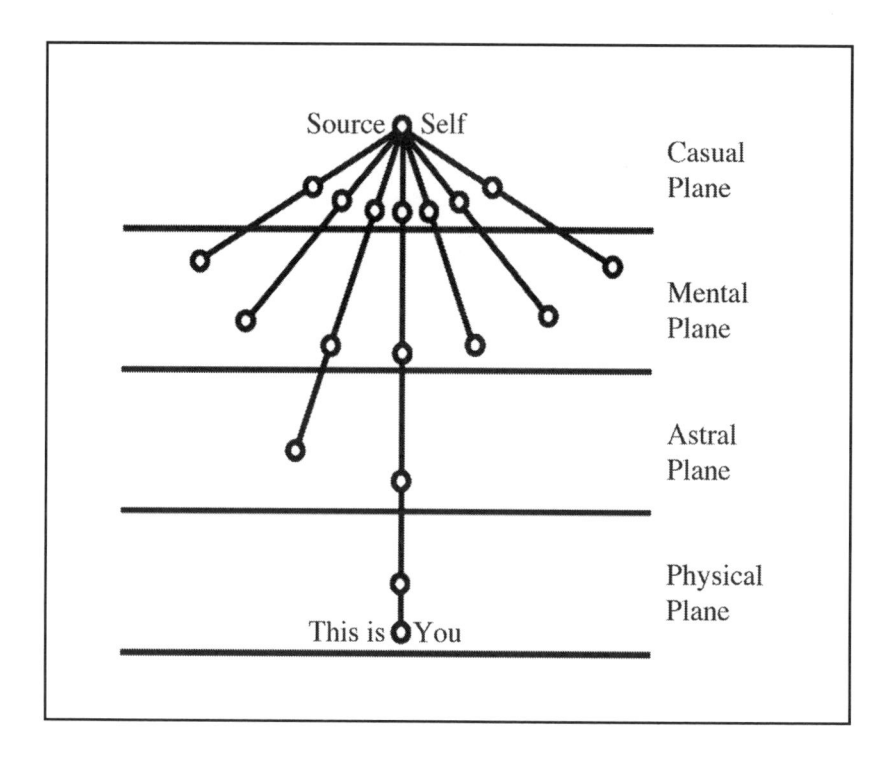

At the same time, your multi-faceted source mind will continue to project seed aspects of itself down into a succession of unique souls, each with an inherited capability that enables them to explore, develop and express their individuality through an increasingly complex range of activity, for as long as you all agree to this.

Lifetimes tend to be grouped in phases of twelve, and your source self has probably sent down many more than just the one set. The more incarnations, the more unresolved issues with the physical experience there will be for your soul group to address before unification is possible.

Even if you, personally, have finished every part of your present destiny assignment, even if you have left behind no negative karma at all, many long-term goals remain unreached. Your source self has aligned its spiritual progress to the development of the sixth plane universe, and you will probably contribute to some further Earth incarnations, from the inner planes, for a long time to come.

## The Advanced Ones Draw Close

At this time of transition into the age of Aquarius, with so many karmic issues clouding the collective vision, many members of the archetypal fraternity have been directing unconditional love into the oversoul of humanity. Spiritually awakened people, wishing to act as channels for higher consciousness, ascended masters and the like, have each attracted a ray from one such archetypal being who can communicate higher truth through them, in much the same way that an aspect of the Christ consciousness was able to overshadow Jesus all those centuries ago. However, many who claim to channel the light aspect of these higher minds are often fooling themselves. They are much more likely to be contacting the shadow of the archetype which, while demonstrating an impressive grasp of occult knowledge, is actually one of the most artful of deceivers.

If you feel you are ready, then attune within your heart to the archetype you sense is linked to you, and then awaken the depths of feeling behind whichever pair of chakras is appropriate, particularly the heart and the throat, the solar plexus and the brow or, when you are ready for this, the crown and base chakras in close accord. With the Master's support, you can draw in the rarefied cosmic streams, those subtle rays emanating from a profound level of the Sun in conjunction with the formative energies beaming up from deep levels of the planet, these two forces blending in a process of mutually spiralling energy.

To be a representative of higher consciousness, to be a 'world server', you must be willing to clear away all those limiting thought patterns that deceive and divert. Balance in all things is the key that a number of well-known mystics could not fully grasp because they wanted to unlock the secrets of the heavens but not the mysteries held within the earth and so, could not mould their dreams into a useful human reality.

We can no longer isolate vital parts of ourselves in this way. We must respect our dual nature and be willing to put in the necessary effort to unify the many strands of consciousness that were conceived and sparked off in early incarnations and which will find their fulfilment in lifetimes to come. That requires us to love every part of ourselves that has ever been, right here, right now, in this eternal moment, for we are already the perfection that we yearn for and suffer for and deny so often.

## The Extent of the Source

Now, let me go back to the beginning and elaborate. It is enough to know that the Source of all existence manifests the essence of creation from nowhere into universe upon universe without end, all within itself.

Every aspect of mind has a dual nature able to project portions of itself to a lower, more extensive reality. You are minute part of the ultimate Father-Mother God, and you are part of the Christ consciousness that operates within it. You are also part of a group soul energy within the Christ orbit. Progressing further down, your own source self, that defines but does not limit your individuality, is a fragment of one of the 'spirit families' that lie within the scope of the group soul, and you are one of the many incarnations initiated by that source self with a certain measure of autonomy.

## Serial Consciousness

The Sun is a many levelled, all encompassing, immensely creative intelligence with an orb of pure light at its core, one part of which is of such burning intensity that the other part must face away, must retreat from it, must hide its rebellious nature from it, if it is to survive. It has been there since the creation of this solar system, and contains the many individual expressions of itself—you, me, everyone. We exist to embody and enhance its dual nature, to reflect its diversity.

The Ultimate Reality dreamed this solar system into being as a part of itself and then rendered itself powerless to directly intervene when all the created life forms, the fragments of its own liberated consciousness, struggled to recognise themselves as beings worthy of unconditional love and respect? With such a limited array of senses available, it is not surprising that we know ourselves only by reflection, attempting to intrude ourselves into apparent outer manifestations of reality—loving, hating, and needing what we perceive as 'other', when there is no outer, really, nothing outside of ourselves, no other.

Your spirit and soul are both orbs with a light and a dark component. You must relate to the dark side of anything with an inner light and to the light with an inner dark. Imagine yourself to be a crystal as used in an old radio set, able to tune into many stations, both long wave and short wave. This particular crystal has not only the ability to receive and pass on rays of light but also, on alternate frequencies, pulses of dark energy. The crystal stays where it is but it can relate to realities far beyond itself, indeed, throughout the entire universe and everything else beyond. That is not really understood yet, and this is merely an introduction.

When aeroplanes first crossed the 'sound barrier', it was necessary to reverse the direction of the joystick, up became down. In the realms between the various planes of existence, similar principles apply. Imagine that a crystal has been placed in the band of transitional energy between the physical and astral planes, and the reality that you are experiencing in your physical body is actually an activity of consciousness sourced from there.

That crystal is yours alone, it is a part of you and, from a point within it that balances many streams of consciousness, it is possible to relate to all the realms, planes, levels, and all activity within and beyond it. One reality can meet another there and interact and, from this, come into a true understanding of the unified nature of all existence. You have 'crystals' between all the other planes, and this explains how the various levels of soul and the spirit interact with each other and how God relates to you.

When you pass to spirit, you have a lot of adjustment to do. You are confined to the border region between the astral and physical planes, taking in elements of both, where you create a replacement reality to the one you've just left, from possibilities that stretch from very bright, vibrant environments that you would associate with heaven, to those that are gloomy and diffuse. This transition environment which resonates intense emotional elements into the human psyche, may now overwhelm you if there is insufficient discipline, and your shadow self could easily hold you into some previous self-destructive behaviour patterns.

Taking the crystal analogy further; all higher beings inter-relate through crystal-like energy of a very complex nature. The four archetypal energies, which originate on the border between the first and second planes, extend down into the lower realms as the elements of fire, air, water, and earth. These are emphasized in different combinations on the various levels. The extent to which they balance within the human evolutionary patterns determines whether the processes that enable form to be established are effectively maintained.

Some people become trapped on the lower astral plane, which is a domain of limited possibilities. The emotional elements in the mind of 'the recently departed' long for a solid body to express themselves through because that is what they have known. However, the band that separates the physical from the astral also provides a suitable environment to orientate the soul to its new field of activity and enable the astral minds to gradually assimilate what it means to be without physical form. Because the astral body is comprised of emotionally motivated streams of energy, it can replicate the feelings that it brought over from the Earth life. The sensuous pleasures are remembered and, all too often, magnified. The sentimental attachments to the physical life need to be dispensed with promptly because they can significantly retard progress if allowed to take hold.

## The Astral Reality

Even though all of the minds and bodies accompanying you on your Earth journey are continually active, prime consciousness is concentrated in the mind that is fully 'awake', that is, both receptive and outgoing. Conscious awareness alternates between adjacent levels, so, during each life, your soul will not only be relating externally through your conscious mind but, using its 'crystal', it can tune into the astral mind when you are asleep. This not only enables expansion of its awareness on that level, but also allows a very creative overview of the life you are leading in your physical reality

When you die and move on to your particular level of the astral world, you will establish surroundings that will be very familiar to you, and you will construct your house there, not with bricks and mortar, but with an in-between kind of substance that is used by your mind to manifest form. This will be your ideal home, with no need of a mortgage. The environment you create will be in tune with your essential nature. After a short period of assimilation, you can take up residence. Though it cannot create truly solid form, the mind nevertheless establishes a relationship to the environment similar to the Earth one.

The music you like will come to you just by opening up to it. The colours you prefer will be all around you. Everything will be according to your emotional attachment to a particular kind of setting, well kept, perhaps, or wild and uncared for. There is no need to invite in anything harsh or unsettling. You can create a heavenly space for yourself, with harps playing in the background, if you wish. But none of this is possible if you have brought with you any strong attachment to an especially discordant way of life.

Those desires that controlled you on Earth will continue to do so. Indeed some people, when they pass, have such a strong attachment to alcohol that it transports their minds back to the places they frequented, and a kind of vicarious pleasure is felt by so doing. They will find themselves unable to live in any heavenly condition while these remain in control. Those who behaved in defiance of the religious teachings they received on Earth, who are now filled with guilt and anger and remorse, are held down into those restrictive attitudes of mind. They might find themselves living in a dark and dank cave or in a kind of limbo.

The afterlife is what you make it and whole groups of people get caught up in a continuation of their human experience. They are held out of time, as it were, and the former relationships and pre-occupations just seem to go on and on without any apparent possibility of change or escape. The mind, in other words, does not allow any kind of higher reality or evolutionary possibility to intrude, for nothing comes to those who do not seek.

In time, such souls will come to realise that their attachment to this restrictive state of mind is retarding their progress. It is not possible to ascend into the higher worlds of spirit while the lower instinctual nature dominates. Any sensation-induced memories of the Earth life claw at the mind, which then retreats into a state of evolutionary inertia.

People who had a very sensual Earth existence, who succumbed to indulgences of all kinds, are often frightened to face, or even to contemplate facing, the wretchedness of what they allowed themselves to become. They push away the feelings of guilt and shame; they deny their inner agony and so, block the way out of their addiction. The Master Jesus invited us to surrender all worldly attachments to follow in his footsteps, but the base human nature that many rely on for their sense of self worth cannot be shaken off any more easily when they die.

There are those, too, of a very devout nature, who believed everything they were told by their religious leaders, that eternal residence in heaven would be theirs if they prayed devoutly and were especially virtuous. Now, here they are in a world that seems to fit that description. They believe that God has granted them the right to everlasting happiness. They are unaware that a higher heaven awaits and, while they continue to hold on to their limited reality, it can take a very long while to move on.

Of course, time does not exist there, but the sense of time passing remains, for it is re-created by the mind. Inevitably, boredom will set in for those languishing in that celestial wonderland, because there is a monotony similar to that experienced on Earth in such circumstances, and little soul advancement. One of the greatest diversions from spiritual progress is through having a too easy life or, in this case, a too easy afterlife, and heaven can be the greatest trap of all.

There are plenty of evangelists in the heavenly worlds who would like to draw these lost ones into their flock, but only those from the higher planes could lead them into a more enlightened reality. These individuals need awakening from their torpor, for nothing of higher matters will impinge until they purge their minds of the desires and complacencies of the past. Only then can something progressive reach them from deep within.

In the early phases of incarnation it will take a long journey, through many lives, before the materially-minded can know themselves as spiritual beings. All their elementary attitudes will be transferred to the astral realms and back again, many times, and they and their communities will experience fire, famine and pestilence, and many will die. They will experience divisions and disagreements that will teach them eventually about loyalty and respect. They will engage in battles with neighbouring tribes, but they will find peace only in nature.

These experiences will lay the foundation for more sophisticated versions later on. Every person has to learn the hard way, through constant repetition, before a release into an expanded, more elevated, consciousness is possible. Until the refined qualities and sensitivities have been properly prepared on the inner levels and then brought through, any new life will be both impulsive and defensive and so, not focussed at all deeply into the true nature of human existence. The essential harmony needed to negotiate life effectively will remain elusive.

Materially orientated souls must eventually face a crisis of faith when the false gods they have created seem to be letting them down and, in some desolate state, a light begins to shine. Only then will the opportunity appear to go beyond the narrow, petty concerns of the self into a more elevated consciousness; but they must be careful that spiritual pride does not develop along with it. The test comes when they are asked, eventually, to unfold a completely honest life, and some will be found wanting. Is that not what is happening today, where many quite advanced souls in positions of power are choosing to direct primitive impulses against the world on a massive scale?

**The Downside of Privilege**
The British royal establishment has been an incredibly resilient fabrication maintained over hundreds of years because, when the powerful ruling elite, the kings, dukes and earls, passed to the spirit world, they built up energy forms that mirrored the hierarchal systems of privilege they had enjoyed on Earth.

Queen Victoria, for example, took up the same elevated position she had known, surrounded by many loyal members of her court. Their enclosed world was transferred almost entirely intact to the astral plane and they were able to sustain this deception because of the deference afforded them by many of their subjects in spirit and on Earth which gave it an assured continuity. Defections from this privileged coterie were few until well into the 1950's.

All of the traditional power structures, parliament, the courts, the various churches, have transferred replicas of their places of authority and influence onto the astral level. It is only now that these are being broken down.

People who had known fame, the admired ones in the arts, the celebrities of earlier days, had no such assured continuity to depend on, they continued to rely on the loyalty of their admirers. Talent has to be constantly renewed on the other side; they cannot rest on their laurels. Edith Piaf, for example, enjoyed an immense affection from the French people and this remains intact because she has continued to develop her considerable ability to link music to the heart.

Also, Marilyn Monroe continues to be adored in spirit. She does admirable work behind the scenes helping those people who have taken their own lives to adjust. When people pass over in this way, they are confused, and you can imagine a visit from Marilyn can be very reassuring because of her immensely warm and generous nature. She reaches out whenever she can to assist those in need, though she is reluctant to come too close to the Earth because of the manner of her passing.

Less talented celebrities lose their followings very easily, for the public are fickle, and it may be that no one welcomes them when they pass. That can make them very embittered and aggressive. "I am important," they think. "People should still be applauding my undoubted talent. I expect it, I demand it." They may come to believe that it is only in a physical body that they will get their following back, the adoration that they feed off, the constant interest in everything they do. It is hard to give this up, but everything of desire in the spirit world immediately creates a resistance and so, these ones are likely to be drawn close to Earth looking for a way back in to re-establish what they had.

**Ignorance has Consequences**
Many people in the West have barely heard about reincarnation. They arrive in the astral world with this ignorance firmly entrenched. Some don't even expect to be there. It doesn't cross their minds that any continuation through a physical body is possible, and no one will enlighten them until they are ready. However, their attraction to the physical experience remains compelling, and they may start to relate to some incarnate people who are open to their advances, and this soon becomes interference.

A possible approach for someone addicted to applause would be to link up with an exciting young performer on Earth who has the same insatiable desire, adding an extra weight of intent, relentlessly spurring that one on, like a possessive parent. Fame is the goal they share. But, when recognition comes, the one in spirit will leach power from the situation to feed his craving.

Unable to be happy just being simply who they are, they have created an ego monster that holds their various bodies down to a very low level. Even quite spiritually mature people can have arrogant personalities that will continue to unbalance them until they are able to cast off the constant self promotion that they carried forward from their life on Earth.

They need to see that there is more to their existence than the approval they receive from others. Quiet discipline is required to break the stranglehold of desire, force never works. In one sense, the challenges they are facing are all illusory, though at the same time, a path must be negotiated through them.

There is another category of people who are held back, the ones who die before their time, in a war perhaps, or by their own hand. Life's unfinished business remains a restriction, a weight that holds their consciousness down. They cannot enjoy a full astral experience until the time is reached on Earth when they were meant to pass. All people have a destiny pattern to adhere to, and the ones who pass as young children will grow to adulthood in the astral realm, surrounded by those who love them. Only then will they be able to lift their awareness onto more mature levels.

Those who have directed their lives more effectively, and are motivated by higher principles, may choose to approach some incarnate person or group on Earth having a spiritual affinity, through the 'crystal' that lies between the astral and mental planes, as a kind of guardian.

**Karmic Restrictions**
In the early incarnation cycles, it could have taken thousands of years before a soul was able to progress to significantly higher realms. Indeed it is possible to return to Earth a great many times without transcending astral consciousness entirely. The lower astral plane contains some very dark and lonely places, and many remain there unable to break a cycle that emphasises the dark hand of the Divine.

People who resonate with a dangerous expression of the left-hand path can be found lurking behind the scenes in some churches where prejudice and hatred are encouraged. They also support those spiritual leaders who trumpet their way as the only one that will gain approval from God, the ones who reject other people's right to discover their divinity in whichever way they choose, the ones who threatened their flock with purgatory or eternal damnation.

The exclusively dark places in the astral world exist wherever the light is not allowed; they exist when the heart is closed or when people cannot face their hidden motives and what they have allowed themselves to become. However, in its purest, most balanced form, the left hand path is not in the slightest bit evil, but few know how to negotiate it safely.

The arrogance of the shadow is intensifying today, expressed wherever human rights are denied, expressed through war and hatred, and the insane notion of 'enemy'. Did not Jesus say, "love thine enemy, as thyself"? And this is even more crucial today than it was in those less sophisticated times.

Much that is dark in the astral experience has been intensified by those Earth lives where the light was not permitted to shine, and also those where the dark was not allowed in to balance the light. Too much light and the soul is blinded. Lives where the dark was forcefully denied led to lives where the light was similarly rejected—another of the paradoxes that is barely understood by most religious leaders.

**Earth family or Spirit family**
In earlier lives, members of the human family were usually members of the spiritual family also. Later on, everyone reaches a point when it becomes necessary to leave the filial family once the karma with them has been completed, and seek out one with a more profound spiritual connection. It may require a move to a quite different locality or country.

This is happening more often today as the strands of the past are woven into the tapestry of the present in all kinds of ways that have not been before. Those awful karmic formations and initiatives of the past, that trapped people in stultifying beliefs and behaviour, are gradually being replaced by alliances formed out of love and mutual support by dedicated souls working in harmony with some vital part of the divine plan.

No matter which 'family' attracts you, you may be sure that there are similar gatherings on the astral level supporting that initiative, and many more of them, too. The closeness of loved ones is one of the greatest joys on that plane, even more so than on Earth, but progress there also eventually requires you to leave a group you have been part of, perhaps over many lives, because their ideas and ways no longer engage you, to gravitate towards one that requires a much more profound involvement.

You may be the first in your group to have felt this kind of stirring, and it can be particularly difficult if no others want to move on with you or, having expressed an initial willingness, they have faltered when the going became tough. However, it is time to relinquish the past and move on to a much more complete existence, and this may require you to sever all contact with the loved ones you are leaving behind.

**The Past Revealed**
There is no sentimentality in the higher spirit realms. There is only what needs to be done. Even so, to step forward alone may, for a time, leave a great hole in the heart, and this is the most common reason why many hold back. But, the pull towards an expanded life is persistent and, eventually, irresistible, and one cannot help but proceed without delay to the great Hall of Incarnations.

This is an energy space of high spiritual intensity and range where it is possible to relive the entire life, not just those events that stood out for you but also, and this can be the difficult part, a full appreciation of what happened to others as a result of your actions, those repercussions that you were unaware of at the time. People are amazed that a thoughtless and unkind act can have resonated so strongly in a friend's soul that it was a contributing factor when, in later years, a state of severe despondency shortened his life. And how a kind act, at just the right moment, had changed the direction of a daughter's life, away from the self-destructive path she was treading, towards a much more satisfying and productive future.

Both are experienced in all their raw and, sometimes, heart-rending emotional detail. Everything is seen for what it was with all the ramifications, and you can understand how shocking this is for people who had lived for the self only.

You may also be shown some details of the very first life which could have been a very primitive, instinctual, nomadic existence. You see that this man had become skilled in the rituals of the tribe and he was very accomplished at tracking down animals for food. He loved to relate stories to the young ones and act out details of the hunt. Yet, despite this, one of his daughters was killed by a wild beast when he was having a heated argument with his partner. So, there is fear of the unknown, tinged with sorrow.

He also developed a strong hatred for another member of his tribe. Then there came a famine when he and his family died. Not a very full life, you might think, but these were the elementary experiences, attitudes and responses that would, in later lives, expand into the qualities and limitations you are experiencing today.

When registering the most significant events of that life, any unselfish support for others would bring a glow, while all those acts that adversely affected the cohesion of the tribe would bring a stunned jolt of recognition and remorse. Most people find that the good deeds outweigh the detrimental ones but, even so, guilt can remain, and this needs to be largely eradicated before grace can come in. It may take more than one visit to the Hall of Incarnations before a full reconciliation between the most recent life and the relevant other past lives can settle into a tranquil heart.

Only then can you reach beyond your astral body and briefly experience what it would be like to be without it, and know whether you are ready to ascend to the plane of the higher mind. In that world of precise mental activity and pure imagination, time hardly exists. It is not exactly that everything happens in the moment, for there is progression, but it is all but instantaneous. It is because that world is not so strongly one of opposites or, rather, there are many kinds of opposites that blend into patterns, quite unlike the simple cause and effect, action and reaction, of the human experience. It is not based in the polarised kinds of separation that are the hallmark of physical activity; there are quite different laws and ways, and everything merges much more without affecting your individuality.

If your own life had been quite a balanced one, then the expansive actions will outshine the heavy, lowering ones when you relive it. You will, perhaps, be greatly surprised at the overall integrity of your life and the positive effect it has had on others. Every time you gave out kind thoughts, or prayed unselfishly to the god of your religion, the power would have gone out and touched the heart and soul of someone in need, and this would resonate strongly now as you systematically examine the details. When the integration of the life is complete, in so far as it can be, you will enter into that state of grace.

Karma is not necessarily expunged by this process, but the surface attachment to the physical life is neutralised so that you can proceed with your journey in the spirit world. Should you be able to progress to the mental plane, it is always quite a lengthy process to adjust to the rarefied thought processes operating there, and it may be quite a while before you can project your mind down through the astral spheres to relate to those you left behind.

No matter where you are in the creation, you can continue to grow in stature and influence. You will continue to develop those aspects of yourself that are appropriate to the level you are on. If you are an artist, you would continue to experiment with the intricacies of colour and form, a scientist would advance his understanding of the laws of creation, a doctor will still have sick souls to tend to and a motherly soul would continue to look after some of the weaker ones in that world, helping them towards a greater maturity. You continue to develop the abilities and interests you had on Earth and this is, I suspect, the way you would want it to be.

In the higher realms, you can make contact with those of your past existences with whom you feel an affinity. The interests of the others may not overlap yours, and you may have little contact with them. Though, when a new life is being planned and their further progress is at stake; they will need to congregate close to Earth and work with you in a team.

At this point, it must be made very clear that there are no absolute rules as to how many lives a source self generates on Earth. It is dependent on individual need. And it is not necessarily true that you can have only one human personality at a time. Even so, there are some cycles of incarnation that apply to the great majority of the human family, working within collective destiny patterns, and it is these I will focus on most extensively.

Also, there are no rules as to how long one must remain and develop in these realms of the mind before the prospect of further incarnation is registered. It is entirely a matter of readiness, and any incomplete things still shot through with earthly desire will be obstructions to a fully functioning life in the worlds beyond. Because of the restrictive force they exert, much of that soul's potential will remain inactive outside a closed mind but, at the same time, the urge to ascend further will continue to build up deep inside.

Or, perhaps you had a successful life, and there is nothing you particularly want to achieve on Earth just now, though, as your perceptions become more subtle and the tone of the Earth quickens, an impulse to experience more will certainly arise later, particularly when members of your spirit family decide to undertake a very important mission together that your oversoul would be very unwise to miss out on.

# 6
# The Next Life

**Between Lives**
When a life ends, the conscious mind goes through the various stages of withdrawal from the human experience, and comes into a state of understanding commensurate with the degree of spiritual evolution it has attained. The sub-conscious mind continues to absorb the energies of harmony and disharmony that flow to it from the soul and from the astral world around, and it registers fresh impulses as they arise from deep within.

The vastness of your inner space is a universe unto itself. At its centre lies your source mind, your archetypal nature, and even before you have passed to the spirit world, it is preparing the next part of itself for the time when this will be projected as shafts of consciousness down through the planes into a new Earth life. It is an ongoing process, and as you and all your former lives continue to feed it with a vast confluence of mental activity, inconsistencies inevitably appear.

In due course, an irritation filters down from the source self, perhaps a sense of stagnation, or something out of kilter with the rest that stems not only from your own life but from other lives that had been. You are never totally separate from any of them though some resonate more strongly with you than others, and it is common to feel a deep fear of retribution for deeds perpetrated by other members of your source group. It takes great courage to take responsibility for separate parts of the overall you that have committed acts of extreme brutality or callousness.

It must be mentioned, that many souls, caught in the grip of guilt, are unaware that forgiveness has already been afforded them by those they harmed, for this knowledge is held back until they are ready to forgive themselves.

There is often a battle going on within the source self between individual parts of itself striving for self determination, and those intent on greater cohesion for the whole. The more lives it has sent out, the more tangled the energies are likely to be in the overall pattern. Many have been away from close proximity to the Earth for a long time and have little memory of it, but they'll eventually become aware that the increasing discomfort within them is due to blockages that can only be released through further physical experience.

A new incarnation is called for and even if you seem to have nothing in common with the others in your band of souls, as the most recent life, and having the clearest link to the physical world as it is now, your participation is essential.

## A New Soul is Prepared

By this time, the seed self that will take on this mission has been further aroused and the dreams of life on Earth have become considerably more vivid. The source mind has drawn the required components from its storehouse of experience and formed them into the strands of aspiration that the spirit-soul combination needs when introducing the essence of individuality into each satellite mind. The strands have only basic form and purpose at this stage but they contain a restrained vitality that will, in due course, carry this potential through into full and harmonious expression wherever it is required.

The procedures to launch a new life have been honed over the many centuries since the introduction of the human species. They are a masterwork of intricate planning in the hands of the spirit elders who have the responsibility to introduce the stuff of destiny into the layered formulations on each level. The most accessible intentions for the life are positioned to be always within the reach of the subconscious mind, but only just.

No matter how strongly the movement towards incarnation is building up, the descent cannot begin until the former lives request it from below. There is nothing forced about it. Once this happens, this new initiative is dispatched down from the source self, recognising that all previous incarnations are, at the same time, continuing to forge their destinies on their respective levels of attainment, without there necessarily being any direct contact or cohesion between them.

**Descent of the Soul**
The first body is generated once the spirit has introduced a nucleus into the accompanying sub-conscious mind and sparked off the life force within it. Only then can an effective link to the embryo be established. There follows a succession of bodies, each needing to be fully alive to its position in the sequence. Representatives of the Lords of Karma will always be there to advise and assist.

Each mind in the sequence needs to feel secure and supported as it acclimatises to the 'atmosphere' of its own level before the next is positioned at a slower frequency. The descent is a natural, almost clinical, process and a high degree of precision is needed to complete it without faltering. No cave explorer would venture into an untried subterranean grotto without first confirming the reliability of the equipment and testing the surroundings for safety every step of the way down.

The bodies are elementary in form and cannot grow significantly until the physical body, the last in the line, has been activated. Otherwise, this would draw energy from the process of completing the chain of consciousness that links them. All of the bodies occupy the same space, and from the moment the embryonic human form begins to develop, the others will remain synchronised to its needs right throughout its life.

Remember, there is a new spirit and a new soul for each incarnation. The spirit part will retain a reasonably clear link with the source self, but the souls of the various lives do not always react well to each other. Free will is already at work, and the semblance of unity diminishes the further they are from the source.

The source self is able to direct purpose through the spirit to the soul right down to the astral level. This could be likened to the two ventricles of the heart pulsating in close accord, and spreading intelligent direction through the energy streams of the entire system. An intuitive process in each mind receives creative and cautionary input according to the needs of its own level of existence, and then passes it on down.

The soul and spirit are fully formed at birth and interpretations of divine purpose are layered within them as a progression of initiatives to be activated sequentially, however, don't forget that there is a dark side to each of them.

Because all the previous lives sent out by the source self still have their higher bodies in place and active, any negative karma that resides on the levels from the astral up, remains entirely with the instigator. Imbalance can occur wherever mind exists, but it is only on the physical plane that karma has to be worked out through a subsequent life.

So, just as the wishes of the source self are transmitted through the spirit into the descending soul, they also filter down through an intuitive receptor in each of its other souls whose issues will influence this new life. There is the initial purity of the new soul and there are the disharmonious energies that will come in after the conception when these earlier lives begin to overshadow the one on Earth.

Free will ensures that errors of judgement usually occur when the etheric body is being prepared because, at this point, all relevant former personalities need to be involved in the process and in agreement, which is not always easy to achieve, and the most recent life usually has the final say.

### Collective Responsibility

Sometimes it takes a very long time for a group of souls to decide to return to the Hall of Incarnations and look back, not just into their own personal Earth excursions, but to see how others of their group had contributed to the various energy blockages affecting them all.

As you saw in the previous diagram, your former lives, as they are right now, are at different levels of spiritual achievement. Each incarnation starts out finely attuned to the central point of the overall spiritual potency of the source self but, while some attract the benefit of higher consciousness, others are dragged down by the weight of the karma they've taken on, and are confused by their inability to deal with what is happening to their efforts and aspirations. Consequently, some souls progress much better than others, both during the life and after.

You may be wondering why the world is so under-populated by people of real stature. Many of the more elevated souls are wisely holding back, leaving the most wayward of our past lives to get behind us as we face the over-riding predicament facing humanity today, which is how to organise ourselves and relate to the planet in a totally new way. These backward ones led us to this moment in time; they created the difficulties that we are having to face and resolve on their behalf. These seem insurmountable at times, and some of us are wondering whether we, and humanity as a whole, have the time left to make up the lost ground.

The highest parts of us are waiting for a more auspicious time to engage in the kind of incarnation we hoped this would be. Yet, our dreams are alive. We still want to leave behind a world where all those who come after will be free to explore its wonders without fear or coercion, and that includes our own future lives. It is not too late for the groups and families to work together. It only requires a little more willingness, a little more compassion, and a little more love each day.

As human ambition tends to settle for the mid-point of what is possible, the more advanced ones around today must put in extra effort to stay with an elevated consciousness in these extremely challenging circumstances. This could be why you feel that no matter how much meditating you do, your freedom to act remains restricted. Some of your earlier lives are possibly holding you back, but it's also due to the reluctance of humanity as a whole to live up to its responsibilities.

Some earlier souls, having spent a long time in the spirit realms, may experience Earth today as a fearful place to approach, particularly where the motives and ingrained resistance to change that led to some of their misdemeanours have been magnified in subsequent lives. Those whose thoughts and deeds were particularly reprehensible may find that, just the thought of facing them again in the Hall of Incarnations evokes fearful images. As each Earth excursion has come and gone, they have repeatedly allowed others in their soul group to have their issues dealt with ahead of them. There is no pressure on any of the lives to face matters of a karmic nature but now, at last, the pressure of their transgressions, building up in the soul, has become unbearable and it cannot be put off any longer.

For a group of former incarnations well in tune with their destiny needs and with a compelling wish to extend their spiritual capabilities, it may be only five years after a life ends before there is another. However, there is nothing fixed in this regard. It takes as long as it takes.

## Visiting the Hall of Incarnations

Let us imagine that you have only been in the spirit world for a few years, yet you are already feeling the need to progress to a higher level. Greater understanding and a willingness to implement it is integral to further evolution, and when you ask to be shown how your existence fits into the overall pattern of lives, you are informed that this exposition could most effectively be undertaken as part of the preparation for the new life that is approaching.

Soon, you hear 'the voice' and, as the one most recently incarnate, you are requested to convene the band of former lives wishing to progress. Some are still in their astral bodies but those with their main focus in the mental body will not have to actually reform their astral self to participate. They project down thoughts that utilize the astral energies.

The group of you are now summoned to the outer chamber of the Hall of Incarnations. Once inside, you cannot rely on the grace that was bestowed on you there earlier. You may have to draw on your deepest inner resources for the courage to face what is revealed this time.

Not all of you can see the communicating entity, but you are asked if you wish to proceed. Are you content with your present existence? Are you satisfied with the work you are doing? Do you wish for a higher elevation of consciousness and a more substantial task to perform? Those indicating "yes" are invited into the Great Hall where they are shown the past—not only scenes from the life that they personally led, but significant incidents from the lives of the others present.

One had been a swordsman who had died fighting a rival clan, and had been in the background of a later life which was as a revolutionary leader in the Balkans. Together, they tried to resolve the matter of taking life by force, but with only limited success. Both would have to be present in the Great Hall for the interlocked nature of this issue to be comprehensively dealt with, but to have deep insight into the spiritual issues involved requires the ability to probe the subtleties with laser-like precision.

Of course, the urge to kill would have had its roots set down even earlier. Any severe blockage or restriction that prevents the present participant from taking effective action will usually have a succession of former lives in the background who contributed to its development. There can be a bewildering array of dubious motives and calamitous behaviour that need to be re-introduced into the destiny plan, but gradually it becomes possible to discern ways to fit it all together. Even so, there will always be buried issues and attitudes that can cause a future life to unexpectedly go astray.

Now, in the Hall of Incarnations you see where each of you made errors of judgement. You are shown incarnations that were meant to lay the foundations for other lives but fell short. You are shown any relevant major incarnations that were entrusted with a mission; and although a great deal was achieved, you can see the opportunities that were missed. Finally, the wasted incarnations are laid bare. Yes, everybody has, at some time or other, had wasted incarnations, and there are likely to be one or two of these in your group.

Then you hear the 'voice' again, asking for your decision. "Are you going to participate behind the scenes of this new Earth adventure and achieve advancement for you all?" Most will say "yes". If any have changed their minds, the process will continue without them and the rest of the synthesis will concentrate on the needs of those willing to proceed.

The ones who said "no", will go back with great discontent because the divine within is digging ever at them. They want to advance but fear has prevailed. However, in due course, when a further life is being prepared, they will find themselves back again saying "yes".

The Lords of Karma can see the cause of everything and know exactly what to present, so that you can, with their help, design a new life that will deal successfully with the issues raised and, at the same time, develop your intuitive appreciation of the greater reality. However, if you are of a somewhat cautious disposition or a tad bit reckless, that will affect your choices.

This enhanced sight can be very liberating but, where there have been great wrongs committed or where a life had consistently not taken advantage of the support offered, despair can cloud the judgement. The greater the picture unveiled, the more the weight of your shortcomings will bear down on you all.

It is very likely that groups from your extended spirit family have already established bases in a number of countries where things had gone awry in the past, but sometimes the location is a new one and there is a special mission to perform there. Perhaps this time you will bring higher ethics into a business incarnation together, or play in the same symphony orchestra.

The Lords have pointed out a number of families where a birth is likely to take place soon, in places where some of those you love and respect also live. They have indicated the kind of life you can expect in these families, and something of where each could lead. You will then be placed in the hands of several of their representatives who will work on the final planning stages with you.

## Decision Time

By now, most of you are aware of how this mission to Earth will affect you, and the decisions that will have to be implemented. You will be made aware of the preparation that has already been carried out. The embryo causal body is firmly in place, as is the mental body. Already, many insights are flowing into them from the spirit that is closely linked to the source self. The embryo astral body has also been generated, but the exact nature of the etheric and physical formation will only be set firm once certain vital decisions have been made.

The background to many of these issues has already been revealed during the time in the Hall of Incarnation, but detail and emphasis have to be defined, particularly the timing for certain pivotal matters to come to the fore. Which sex will the earthly body be? What special characteristics will it have, and what are the exact details of the destiny plan that need be woven into the fabric of the etheric consciousness to support this human life?

So, you and all those with a stake in these decisions meet up with the representatives of the Lords of the Karma who've been closely involved in the preparation process and understand the issues well. Several former lives, with greater awareness, will wish to be instrumental in the planning for altruistic reasons. You like them immensely and you elicit their help to proceed in an orderly fashion through the negotiations ahead. Alas, there are a couple with less spiritual understanding who seem to have missed the point entirely, and they are by far the most forceful of the bunch.

**A Life Contemplated**
To construct a detailed blueprint for a new life, all the issues have to be sifted through and linked to specific higher directives. It will contain a range of relationships and soul developments that can fit together into a unified pattern. Much will be discarded. It may be that one life will have to miss out altogether.

Everything must respond to the collective will that accompanies the birth, but several who did not get everything they wanted from the Hall of Incarnations may still be trying to exert undue influence over the final planning process, and it is a concern that you might be pressured into ignoring some of the advice given by the Lords of Karma.

These most patient of beings have made their suggestions, based on what they know to be the needs of the source self but, in the end, they can be overruled, and the tactics used to coerce the sensitive ones into giving ground will involve the same kind of manoeuvring and one-upmanship that occurs in any decision-making group on Earth. You will have to assert your principles. A strong inner conviction on every issue will be the deciding factor.

When the source self is more mature, many of the lives can understand the deeper implications and will respond constructively to any advice given. However, when the passions of the Earth consciousness rise up again, when the past intrudes too much, even then, good intentions can fall by the wayside and poor choices are made. You will need to take your role of convener very seriously indeed.

**Major and Minor Lives**
Every so often in your cycle of incarnations the very best needs further expression and, provided the disruptive traits can be put aside when expressing that gift, everything will proceed as planned. An opera diva could not afford to let wayward emotions get the better of her, or a concert pianist. There must be an almost steely focus on the task in hand.

Sometimes an old soul has developed a particular skill to a very high degree and an incarnation to display that mastery is decided upon. Mozart, for example, was a master of music and he brought a very long history of musical expertise with him that he was able to access at an early age. You don't become a master at your first attempt.

Now, there were other things in him that clearly weren't so accomplished; temperamentally, he was almost a child in some ways. His music needed great emotional sensitivity and it had to come through a passionate heart. A rigorous determination was needed to put his emotional instability aside when channelling the high quality of music that his mastery allowed him.

If he had come to work on his emotions, he couldn't have created music at that level. He would have chosen a life where he plunged himself repeatedly into challenging emotional situations until he could achieve harmony in all those inner places where disharmony had been.

The musical part of the Mozart oversoul would not bother to

incarnate today. He would want to compose music on a much more refined level. In such discordant times, few would welcome it. Music is a potent force on this planet, but music of that vibrancy would cause far too much shadow to rise up in the soul of humankind and he would have to be silenced.

People are crying out for the return of a great Master teacher, but would he be really listened to? Beings of that high stature are never loud and brash. They would not bother to go on television or organise great rallies; and how do you think Jesus' message "Give up all your worldly possessions and follow me" would be received in the halls of power? He would ask the Catholic Church to sell up their land and give the proceeds to the poor. "Now just a minute, Jesus, you can't really be suggesting that you want your places of worship sold off." "Yes," he would say, "Do it in my name."

Clearly, it is not yet time for such elevated souls to appear. They are waiting in the higher realms until the intense karmic confusion of these times is dealt with, until the turmoil subsides and we are ready for what they would wish to teach us. Humankind has much to learn and resolve first.

Not all lives are full of expansive activity and great leaps forward, some consolidate or are preparatory. So, is this to be a major life or not? It is a motley crew you are faced with and so, this new soul is certainly not going to be a high spiritual teacher or a creative genius. In any case, in a number of your recent lives, the artistic gifts were developed to quite a high degree and it is not uncommon for the next one to attend to some of the less developed attributes in mundane settings. This assembled group includes several that did not achieve much because their lives came to an end before the allotted time, and there is one who left the area of relationships undeveloped in order to explore a love of botany to a high degree. The woman he was meant to marry is a likely participant in the coming life.

A list of priorities is made, and at the top is the choice of a male or female body. Looking at the eight lives vying most strongly for inclusion, it is significant that six were male but then, men usually incur the most visible karma, don't they? Obvious, too, is a strong chauvinistic behaviour running though most of them, where their partners had been loved because they fulfilled a social or domestic function rather than for themselves alone. The sexual drive was strong and invasive, and ruthlessness in business stands out, too. Sport was prominent, but the more sensitive artistic gifts were rarely developed. Their children were regimented into forced patterns. The parents in old age were invariably neglected. Although there had been many lives in religious settings, they had not entered fully into the spiritual aspects of the teachings in any of them. The rituals had been practised but not deeply understood. Now, that is quite a lot to be going on, isn't it?

**The Major Lives**
Usually the three most significant lives are selected to be the overarching ones for the life ahead, but two can be settled on if they are particularly extensive or difficult. Four major lives are usually too much of a burden for most people to handle. Some attempt it, but they usually regret the decision.

The effects of these three lives are extensively woven into the destiny pattern. It is not usual to be dealing with all three at a time, but they will be there as strong background factors throughout the life, coming and going in emphasis as required. Together, they contribute the most significant issues to be faced. The influences of other lives will come in for shorter periods or through special relationships, but these will be less important overall.

The first life in a particular trio that we are going to study in some detail was a slave-trader in Egypt at the time of Rameses II. He went to the occupied territories and purchased fit males and nubile women that he thought would please the members of the ruling elite. He treated his charges very poorly. Money was his god, and he drove a hard bargain. Initially, he acted well towards his wife; she and the family did not want for the necessities of good living, but his interest waned when she grew older and lost her looks. He then used younger, more attractive girls for his pleasure, particularly one who was a personal servant to his wife. He had two children, but much more love and attention was lavished on the boy than the girl.

The second life was as a Roman centurion. He was a favourite of the Emperor and was very accomplished at dispatching Christians. He particularly liked the attention he received from the ruling class. He never married, but formed a very close relationship with a fellow centurion and was shocked when his friend was killed in the arena. This started him thinking about the value of this kind of life, but the acclaim kept him going. Eventually, he, too, was killed, at the age of 35.

Then there was the life in India, the second son of the Maharaja, who believed he deserved to become the ruler, rather than his rather ineffectual elder brother. He cleverly inveigled himself into his father's confidence and became indispensable in the handling of his financial affairs. However, when the old man died, his brother still ascended to the throne.

Resentment grew in him, and he was greatly relieved when his brother fell out with the palace guards and died in an uprising. However, instead of being called on to take over, his teenage nephew was made ruler with a cousin acting as regent. He was transferred to oversee an outlying province and died a bitter man.

He started out as a good family man but, because of his narrow and overbearing ambition for them, his two sons eventually became estranged. The elder became a swami in a nearby religious community, while the younger married well and moved away to a neighbouring province.

Now, should the new life be male, incarnating into a body and a family situation that would encourage these chauvinistic tendencies to surface, or female, in order to learn what it is like to be at the receiving end of the same things that he meted out in former lives as a husband, father or employer?

You either re-establish the extreme behaviour in a way that helps you deal with it, or confront the issues in a converse situation. It is not unusual for a former slave owner to incarnate later into an African-American body; this kind of reverse experience is an option to consider here.

After a very short deliberation, a male body is chosen. The

intricacies of the life must now be carefully decided. Having become aware of every significant experience in the relevant former lives, it is possible to sense the future to the same extent. That is a spiritual law—balance in all things. However, it is the weight of the past that concerns you. To take on too great a burden would swamp or even disintegrate the fabric of the new life because the limited Earth mind cannot carry too much at once. You cannot overload the electrical system without a fuse blowing. In the same way, it is unwise to overload the human mind with too much complexity.

The soul, having no previous experience of physical life, will have only a limited understanding of what is being decided on its behalf, so it is reliant on the advice given. But it does need to respond where it feels something is inappropriate and express this dissatisfaction by a form of telepathy. Its first major evolutionary step may be to trust the inner promptings and resist any undue pressure being applied by former lives defending their corner.

**Establishing the Qualities**
Childhood is the formative stage when past attitudes and unresolved issues need to be introduced in very elementary forms. If it is seen that jealousy came up regularly in other lives, situations would be arranged where this emotion is aroused—starting with jealousy of a brother or sister who seems to be getting more love and attention—and then as a young adult in a love relationship where the partner flirts outrageously.

Procrastination is another issue and, at school, there will be deadlines, and engaging in sport would require swift reactions. In every life, there are always many awkward tendencies to be smoothed out and misguided attitudes rectified. These are usually signalled early on without necessarily needing to be addressed at the time. Their outworking will be staggered in the destiny pattern. As one issue is resolved, another that has been there in the background, barely noticed, but a chance meeting causes it to rise strongly to the surface. It is not until outside circumstances pull these compromised energies to the fore that they can properly be dealt with.

So, it is necessary for him to meet certain people or kinds of people, who will highlight the issues to be faced and provide the challenges that will give the stuck energies a jolt, allowing the psyche to rebalance in a more subtle manner. Zest for life will bring forward any creative talents that need further development, in art, music, the theatre or through the psychic gifts. Progressing these more sensitive attributes is of equal importance to grappling with the material restrictions caused by karma, the two need to be worked on side by side.

**What kind of parents?**
If a man had been a particularly ineffectual parent in a former life, then a weak father may be chosen to help him understand the affect this has on a child's upbringing, so that, when he has a youngster of his own later on, he will be able to bring up this sensitive soul in a firm and much more supportive way.

On the other hand, he might have to contend with a harsh father to arouse the need to be stronger, more resolute, and able to stand up to him, to be his own man. This inherited weakness will then turn into a confident self belief that will open doors for him later on. There are always these opposite alternatives, but the one taken up will be largely determined by the choice of parents available.

Of course, it would seem to be unwise for a child to have a father who would dominate so strongly that the potential in that one is completely squashed. But, a total inversion of the previous life situation may be the only way to address the harshness existing between them. Some children find themselves in quite horrendous situations but there is always a reason for it. Karma may be that severe. An adult could walk away, of course, but a young child does not have that option, so it is very important to get the family surroundings just right.

The parents are chosen to provide the experiences that the child needs. Their beliefs, attitudes, and prejudices, and the amount of unconditional love they can give are all important. These early influences will either be taken on or rebelled against; and the manner of their responses will determine the strength of the child's resolve to move strongly into maturity, or be a victim of circumstances.

A mother may seem to be a most desirable person on the surface, but it would be disastrous if the soul were to enter, only to find that she is not so beautiful after all and an abortion is needed. Though, it would teach him to be more careful in the future. The Lords of Karma had known all the likely consequences, but their advice to delve more deeply was brushed aside.

## The Lords of Karma do not Lie

Not everything is revealed to you by the Lords of Karma. Until there is a depth of understanding, you would not be able to discern with sufficient clarity why a particular path should or should not be taken. The clues will be there, but until you can ask questions such as, "If this action is taken, won't this be the outcome and shouldn't I, therefore…?" the implications may not be seen until after the incarnation has begun when things start to go askew. It will then take some deep soul searching to avoid a crisis.

The Lords are not allowed to present anything beyond a person's ability to understand, accept, and make use of. They do not lie but they only dispense the amount of information they feel is necessary. Advice is only proffered when it is specifically asked for.

For example, those needing to be born in Germany in the early 1920's as Jews might have felt that war was finished and a rosy future would open out for them. A warning would have caused them to incarnate elsewhere, outside of their karmic field. Where doubts were expressed, the Lords of Karma may have said "Well, there is this other set of parents in Poland that you might like to consider," and the karma would not have been sidestepped after all. They are there to give options and to help focus in on things that need to be done irrespective of how difficult they may turn out to be.

Even then, nothing was inevitable, for when war approached, people made quite different choices. Some were so attuned that they were able to step away from the holocaust to come, while others stayed to face their destiny. It is impossible to predict what is going to rise up from the depths of any soul in a time of crisis.

In their earlier lives, people don't understand very much at all. If they are not mature enough to understand the ramifications of their decisions, then it doesn't matter, for everything is useful experience. But, those in later lives who don't bother to probe under the surface could be in for some nasty surprises as things proceed. Inner illumination will only come when it is reached out for—those sudden glimpses of what lies ahead, accompanied by the clear sight needed to manifest the essence of it smoothly into the life.

It would be of no use to give a child a sum to work out with the answer alongside. In a similar way, the Divine Consciousness, in whose hands are the keys of knowledge, in whose minds are the streams of wisdom, in whose heart there is infinite compassion, and in whose essence are the charts of eternity, will never take away your right to self-discovery and self-determination.

The plan would be wrecked if we could look backwards and forwards beyond our capability to assimilate. The Divine Couple who filled this Universe with individual expressions of their love, who created the ultimate destination of each human soul, needed to do no more than that. What rests in our deepest levels of being is complete, and needs no elaboration, no reformation, no outer approval, as we children of the ethers will discover in our own time. When our inner child reaches adulthood, the ability to invoke the memory that belongs entirely to that inner life is offered to us all.

It is usual for higher understanding to remain firmly in the background until certain events have opened the conscious mind to a more enlightened perspective. Each revelation must touch the highest and lowest parts of us, and flow through to the etheric and physical forms without disturbing the equilibrium too much. This allows new initiatives to unfold in precisely the right order and context.

**Decision Time**
Eventually, the time comes to decide which parents will provide the most favourable opportunities for spiritual growth. It is rarely a

foregone conclusion. It is natural to gravitate towards people from former lives, some with stronger links than others, and the Lords of Karma take this into account when presenting the available alternatives. The most intimate past contacts may not throw up any to choose from and they will have to venture out into a wider pool of soul affinities to find any that would fit. During the past twenty incarnations there were forty parents and double that number of grandparents but some of these were repeats. There were brothers and sisters, and children and marriage partners, and their in-laws, and many intense short-term relationships. Add to this some past business partners, nannies, and so on. Perhaps, six hundred altogether.

The Lords search through this contingent. Not many are of a child-bearing disposition and able to provide a compatible environment and upbringing, so the possibilities are quickly whittled down to only a handful. Further refinement is necessary to discern which will most closely fit the requirements. It could be that one family will contribute a particular range of influences, and another would provide a quite a different mix of the required ingredients.

The couple chosen has to provide the necessary training for the child to grow up confident and well directed, with reservoirs of simple accomplishment built up early on, that can be added to as it progresses into the adult challenges that must follow.

Deeper issues cannot be addressed until the appropriate lines of destiny have been activated, but preparatory work can be done at any time. Perhaps there is something that a previous soul had backed away from when the going became tough, so the child must learn to stick with any fears and resistances that arise. Courageous decisions taken in childhood can stand a person in good stead when tackling more difficult situations later on.

Past relationships are not necessarily played out in exactly the same roles. Parents become children, siblings become business partners, and teachers become students. The possible combinations are endless. It can come from anywhere in the scope of past incarnations, just as long as the issues being worked on by all participants dovetail in.

## More Detail for the Life

To illustrate this further, let us return to the three major lives that we will study in detail, the Egyptian slave trader, the Roman centurion, and the Maharaja's son. These have been confirmed, and the sex of the body designated as male. The preparation of the etheric body can now proceed, and the physical body that will follow on from it.

In the end, there are only two couples that fit the bill and who want a child at this particular time. In one of these, the husband was the father in Egypt. The ruthless skills in the marketplace that the new soul will inherit were learnt from this man, who is now an African-American living in Florida and married to a very caring white school teacher—a very motherly type with whom there has been little contact in past lives.

The wife in the other couple is the sister he had been very fond of in Rome. In this life, she is married to a strict Presbyterian preacher in Scotland—again, not someone who featured much in other incarnations, although he was one of the Christians that the centurion put to death.

If neither of the suggested couples is chosen, the Lords of Karma will point out other possibilities that could become available later on. You can already see what a complicated business it is to sort out a new life that will be productive for all concerned. Both possibilities will provide a range of useful experience within the family, extending to friends at school and those other members of the spirit family living nearby.

In early incarnations, most related souls come together in the same village or in a tight-knit religious community. It would be very difficult to avoid meeting up with them. Today, substantial numbers of your extended family may be incarnate in four or more different locations, with everyone gravitating to where their karma is. It is not uncommon to be born in one place that fits the bill for the time being, only to move later to another that provides more advanced opportunities and relationships. In other words, you may have to leave your earthly family to meet up with your spiritual one.

So, it is back in the Hall of Incarnations where the Lords confirm the two couples intending to have a child in the near future, and they reveal details of the past lives of all four of the prospective parents, explaining the ways in which they are suitable.

The Florida one first: the father, chauvinistic of course, from a born-again religious background, an amateur baseball player when young but now just a spectator. It is likely he will have heart problems later on and may need support from his children then. The family is quite poor due to a failed business venture and this could stimulate in our man, an almost fanatical desire to succeed in business, inherited from the earlier Egyptian life. The potential mother will provide a very strong moderating influence in what will be a very difficult father-son relationship. There are no other children yet, but it is likely, though not certain, that a sister will come along within a couple of years who was the favoured female servant in the Egyptian life.

In Florida, some of the people he had supplied slaves to in Egypt and who were also members of the ruling class in India, will become business associates in this. As most will come from wealthy white backgrounds, he will experience difficulty in overcoming his race and upbringing to make progress. To be accepted into the influential business community will become an obsession with him, and the spiritual quality of the methods he uses to achieve this will define his life.

Now, on to the Scottish situation. His elder brother here was his Maharaja father in the Indian life, but also the fellow centurion he adored in the Roman one. In order to break away from his strict Christian upbringing, the brother will move first to London, where he will attend University and graduate in bio-genetics. He will take a job in Florida and, later on, will invite his brother there to work with him. So, there are two possible routes to the same destination. Obviously their mutual dislike of Christians would be emphasised in both environments.

He will not marry until he reaches Florida, and it will probably be the wife from the Egyptian life, now in a mixed race body, and promiscuity will again be an issue. Who will his children be? This is more problematical, because promises made twenty five years before the time are not always adhered to. Enough to know that many members of his close family of souls are already incarnate in Florida, or soon will be, and a smaller number in Scotland, so either life would be well positioned from the outset.

However, a problem has arisen. There are other souls wishing to incarnate through these particular parents. The Florida couple is especially in demand. All the applicants are considered and there is one particularly determined contender who does not want to give ground. As the Scottish route is the easier, in all respects, this is chosen. The astral consciousness of both intended parents gives its assent and the process moves forward to its final phase.

# 7
# When Life Begins

**Difficulties Ahead**

So that we can explore the complexities, I have assigned you the role of bringing this new life into being. Misunderstandings may snarl up the planning from the outset where many of the former lives have been away from physical existence for a long time, and the pace and circumstances of life have changed out of all recognition. If you travel a lot, you know how difficult it can be to adjust to the social restraints and lifestyles found in some countries and these former personalities may very well misjudge the pressures of modern urban living where life is not centred around the family. The moral freedoms enjoyed in today's secular society will be particularly challenging.

It is never easy to formulate the intricate patterns of potential that will be layered, phase upon phase, into the subtle etheric field, particularly when you choose a body of the opposite sex. These need to unfold precisely in their turn yet be immensely flexible. If you remember how tough your own childhood was, your decisions may be overly cautious. On the other hand, if life unfolded easily, you may not expect a world where complacency and moral laziness are encouraged. Without proper discipline, the greed factor will inevitably arise to undermine your progress.

The soul itself may be unduly attached to the rarefied environment of the source and it may not wish, when the time comes, to descend into close contact with the dense, dark influences of the subterranean Earth. But the Lords of Karma have made it perfectly clear that this is an essential part of your evolutionary journey, that returning 'home' is not an option. In your decisions for this new life, you are naturally determined that everything faced will be achievable and satisfying.

## The Final Preparations

The choice of family has been made and the exact location and early influences are in place, but before unanimity is reached, challenges arise. One of the former male lives is trying to use force to override consensus. While claiming good intentions, he constantly frustrates and blocks those who wish to follow the detail of the advice given. "Don't listen to them," he says, "What do they know?"

The Lords of Karma, in whose minds are the crucial keys to understanding, in whose hearts the true way is revealed, cannot give advantage where none has been earned. They will not try to stop you if you choose to step out of line. Options are presented and they offer their advice, but ultimately it is left up to you, the most recent life, to decide which components are to be worked on in collaboration with those other souls vying to be represented on Earth by this coming incarnation.

The further into the process, the more likely you will see with unnerving clarity, the stringent demands of the tiers of destiny needing to be enacted and the backlash energy that some of you will have to absorb and endure.

When the detail has been settled, the astrological patterns are prepared, incorporating a precise configuration between the elements of fire, air, water and earth that will ensure the form, strength, and longevity of the physical body. The distillations of destiny are organised and woven energetically into layered patterns within the DNA. But, once achieved, the Lords will step back and watch over the further proceedings with great humility.

At the same time, others of their hierarchy are visiting the guardians of various members of the extended spirit family that they hope will interact with the child in its early life, and those who could play significant roles later on. There is so much to be attended to before the descent into the womb of a welcoming Earth mother can be completed.

The spirit-soul relationship establishes individual purpose in body after body on the way down. The soul needs to find balance in all parts of itself if it is to stay in close harmony with the spirit, for as it descends into heavier, more distant environments, this cohesion is increasingly upset by outer influences. So, the soul needs to be tactically very astute in influencing the will of the human consciousness as it responds to the lure of life.

Free will effectively means that the lower decides for the higher, but problems may still occur when the basic detail formulated by the band of former lives is introduced into the etheric consciousness or, more crucially, when the required soul portion extends its range to engage the heavy nature of the physical experience at the moment of conception.

It is a new soul on probably its one and only visit to the planet. The preparation for this moment has been through the dreaming process, but the reality may provide quite a shock. The light coming in from the source is simple and precise. The dark brings infinite capability. It remains the unpredictable side of human existence, and this is why so many people fight to exclude or contain it.

The soul has been vibrating in relative harmony with the light and dark aspects of the spirit, spiralling in and spiralling out, and now, suddenly, it seems as if the light has been shut off as a slower frequency is impulsed into it from its own dark side, which drags it down. The dark momentarily assumes control and the soul is then confounded by energies coming up from below in very unexpected ways.

The dark energy is the generator of what happens when the soul opens up to accommodate what it must become in a much more complete way. The base self has asserted itself, and with a spirit impulse coming in to balance it, these two rapidly alternate, sparking off a creative dynamic between its etheric and physical levels that lasts until the soul rebalances at the slower frequency necessary for human existence, the dark and light, for a split second, in perfect harmony.

## Completing the Process

This procedure will establish the response mechanisms and the motivation for the kinds of activity needing to be undertaken in the physical guise. At this moment, responsibility is handed over to the conscious mind and then, crucially, impulses from deep within the Earth reveal to the soul the heavy nature of the karma it must address.

This sparks off the growth of the etheric body and also draws in the materials from the surrounding environment that will consolidate as the physical form. The embryo begins developing from a state of harmony and the destiny energies being released will allow the subtle material being directed into the soul from the source self to 'breathe'.

The time of birth has been set to connect up exactly with the beneficial influences from the planets and their progressions. That is why so many children come from the womb at unexpected times, they're 'late' or they're 'early', because they are trying to fit into the chosen pattern. So often you have doctors and nurses, who understand nothing of the natural way, trying to stimulate the birth to suit their conceptions. There is always the perfect moment for this to happen.

Sometimes the baby is interfering with the natural flow. It may be having last moment doubts, or it may be anxious to be there as quickly as possible to start its experiences. If it isn't responding to the natural rhythms, entry into life will be awkward. There could be reluctance in the mother, for this birth will require her to give up some of her freedoms to look after the child. All sorts of factors determine whether the pregnancy culminates on schedule.

Within the womb, getting the growth phases to proceed in harmony with the etheric form is an intricate process, for the embryo is a little bit at the mercy of circumstances. At this particularly chaotic time in Earth affairs, there is always the possibility of mass free will interfering with plans, leading to an accident, so-called, but, in reality, it is a result of interference. The mother falls over and the shock interrupts the process, so the foetus aborts.

Those who oversee the birth from the spirit side have to be constantly near the situation so that, at any moment, they can introduce new energies that will help growth to proceed naturally. If there is an unexpected illness, such as scarlet fever or the mother unwisely takes certain medicinal drugs, emergency action may have to be taken. However, even though the conditions are not perfect, it may still be worth going on. Adjustments are being made right up to the time of the birth.

You can be sure that, regardless of whether you follow their guidance, the representatives of the Lords of Karma will accept the decisions made and do all they can to implement them. They are well aware that their own ability to see into the essence of things is not the absolute. No one can possibly know what lies in the deepest reaches of your being other than the Ultimate Mind that created you.

**A Life is Terminated**
Any consideration of when life begins raises questions about the spiritual validity of abortion. The moment of soul connection is adaptable, for if the foetus is discharged some weeks into the pregnancy, this final link in the chain may not yet have been firmed up and the line of subtle bodies can still access a replacement incarnation through the same or a different mother.

However, in certain circumstances, an abortion, spontaneous or otherwise, will result in the termination of this physical life and the embryonic individual will grow up in the spirit world in much the same way that it would have done on Earth, without there being a further attempt at incarnation. It is then that induced abortion may have severe karmic implications for the ones who carry it out—not only the parents, but the medical team that perform the termination. However, nothing is clear cut; in these matters, motive is everything.

Assuming that the life continues to develop as planned, the string of elementary bodies occupying the womb space must adjust to the energies reaching them from the worlds they will eventually inhabit. Following the moment of conception, the causal body begins growing in its particular fashion, accompanied by its aspects of mind, as do all the others. The oversoul participates in the whole process through its two emissaries, the spirit and the soul, and it is usually quite a smooth process, with expert support supplied right down the chain of consciousness.

## When Life Begins

The first phase of the destiny plan generates many of the basic growth elements that will underpin the life, but the purposeful energies that are activated initially within the etheric formation are of far greater strength than the physical part would seem to require in the very early days. Some of these energies are pumped out by the active pulse of destiny into the subtle levels that lie just outside range of human consciousness, eliciting responses, both progressive and restraining from the people around, and these impact on the foetus.

This will determine the parents' responses to the coming birth. If there is karma with the mother, a subliminal resentment may be there. She may feel a duty to the child but no warmth. Does she look after her body so that the right nutrients flow to the foetus, giving it a good start? Does she give up smoking and drinking heavily? Does she exercise properly? These decisions are swayed by the karmic energies coming from the etheric foetus. Also, how willing she'll be to put aside her weaknesses on behalf of the baby within her depends on the influences allowed in from her own former lives.

In so many ways the baby is already receiving a response to the karma it has brought with it. And, though not all of the issues will need to be dealt with early on, the former lives, by their presence and the mental projections they are sending down, are establishing some very crucial core reactions in the elementary form.

Psychologists assert that much that is obstructing an adult life can be explained by those early experiences in the womb, right through a traumatic birth process into the early years. One parent may be celebrating the arrival of this child and is eager to support it, while the other is having doubts. Their thoughts and attitudes affect the ability of the foetus to accept the past life experiences still active within the deep confines of memory and, where they are inadequately assimilated along the way, these inherited factors may break out later in quite convoluted forms.

Right up until the moment of birth, wayward forces and unforeseen events can divert the process away from the harmony needed for the launch. However, the soul, which has the overarching brief to stimulate life and purpose into each level within its jurisdiction, will certainly be attempting to consolidate the relationship between the bodies and their minds, from the very vibrant mental responses to the slowest activity at the physical extremities.

**Following the Birth**
All former lives chosen to be major players behind the scenes of the coming incarnation will have made their commitment clear. You and they are required to remain close to the incoming child during the time in the womb and for three years after, until the basic ingredients of that life are fully established. It is a joint responsibility. Free will allows any of you to break that agreement, but it will be to your detriment if you do.

Although some of the former lives are initially mere background players, it is likely that a few have karmic issues with one or both of the parents—an old adversary, perhaps, or a jilted lover—and the past personalities of any participants with grievances to express will be creating friction on the astral plane which will filter down.

When you consider all the levels involved, life on Earth is a very complex procedure. The fledgling soul is, initially, not too caught up in the outer reality on each of the levels it occupies. This naivety is necessary because, in the first three years, the physical and astral worlds need to intermingle. When there is a psychic openness, the guardians and higher ones appear to the baby with beautiful sightings of the heavenly worlds, comforting images, but a few with a particularly severe karmic load see monsters, too. This is very much a case of karma returning to bless them or haunt them.

Beyond the third year, the natural desire for more experience takes over and most of the conscious connections with other levels of itself will fade away. They are replaced by an outer world that the child really doesn't understand very well.

Right from the beginning, the highest aspects of its consciousness give off, through the etheric self, the kind of energy that invites favourable responses from the surrounding environment. The inherited karmic energy is sending out its own attractions. These responses will inevitably clash, generating conflict around the child or some form of neglect.

A very young child is already living a very extensive life on the subliminal levels and this is preparing the way for the adult life to come. Indeed, the first three years of a baby's development leaves a jumbled storehouse of emotional reflexes, some expansive, some uncertain, that sharpen or blunt the growing awareness. Times of elation are experienced, pure connections to the world are acutely felt, alongside the fears and irritations, frustrations and disappointments, all of which mould the temperament and the response mechanisms that, of course, are linked to the former lives that are coming close.

**Destiny Revealed**

Then, the apparent separation between self and everything else increases and, after a few more years of partial connection between the worlds, a curtain is effectively drawn between them. Trial and error becomes the way of life.

Sometimes, the baby realises that it is not ready to cope and withdraws, leading to a very introverted childhood later on. As it grows older, the nuances of the destiny plan are progressively activated and it is the maturity of the response to these energies that will determine whether the child has the courage to deal with the challenges they represent. If it continues to shy away, that is probably because it senses the karma ahead, the harsh experiences it may be forced to go through.

Your human consciousness relates mainly via the senses. Your sub-conscious mind reaches to include part of the etheric awareness, and to set up an effective working relationship between the two you must develop on an intuitive level.

Operating through the lower chakras requires discipline, for the pure does not always know how to handle the impure, any more than the impure knows how to handle the pure. When the higher and the lower elements are balanced in the heart, encouraging resonances from the spirit can be accessed.

Some youngsters develop an over-confident ego when influenced by a former life of privilege, such as from that high-born

Indian family we are considering. A sense of importance is there, with the expectation that everything will unfold at the flick of a finger. However, if the parents hold back their love, which they may well do, and the child is bewildered, it goes against all expectations. It may scream and stamp and hit out in protest. This rebellious behaviour is usually the result of a deep inner frustration that masks feelings of inadequacy and unworthiness, and any resentment held on to will cause the youngster to underachieve or be overcome by insatiable desires.

**The Life Unfolds**
Every soul gravitates to what was established in the past and then is inclined to reinforce the status quo; but life today will not let us get bogged down in a comfortable existence for long. Even where a baby is in a situation that is meant to fulfil its requirements exactly, there may be much unexpected discord coming in from those around.

Indeed, some find that it's just too much for them, and they end their life prematurely in a cot death or, if it persists, by taking their own life later on. This is usually an ego thing. "I am special. I thought I could do this but the support I need just isn't here and I'm unable to cope." Well, there is no choice but to go on and learn from having over-reached, having misjudged the challenges, by working through the reactions and resistances that occur, so that it won't happen again in quite that way.

Despite this, you are not alone in generating what happens in your life. There are many members of your spirit family manoeuvring themselves towards you on many levels. There is also support from your 'guardian angels' acting under direction from on high. They are part of a vast collective reality that you can relate to only indirectly via the displaced resonances of their presence.

And so, gradually and painstakingly, life develops exactly as it needs to with you as the main attraction. Today, the concerns of the human ego remain persistent and most people are caught up in the unreality of it all. You live in a world frequented by people who are, in the main, not like you. Many of them are quite spiritually backward, you might think, a bit simple.

Primitive man lacked all the refinements that modern man enjoys today—he did not need them. Social structures today and the ways of relating to them have to withstand a much faster, more intense energy bombardment, and this requires mature responses that could only have been developed over great tracts of time. You may sometimes wish you could return to those uncomplicated earlier situations but, of course, you probably wouldn't enjoy it if you did. You must find your simplicity in the present, for you are, in truth, absolute simplicity.

**Difficulties Are Encountered**
Even one step on your life's journey can be quite daunting, and this is not surprising when you consider that your other bodies and their attendant minds are subjected to many harsh influences and challenges outside your range of awareness that impact on you. These reflect the Earth's current turbulence and the part you played in bringing it to that state.

There are energies filtering down from your source meeting those coming up from the earth at a precise point that has hidden depths. It requires pure inspiration and an enlightened attitude to access the power of this effectively. To complicate matters, some of your more wayward former lives, gathered around and linked in, are sending resonances of their past misdeeds down through you into the earth. This is attracting responses from the storehouse of karma lodged there.

If you resist these past impulses coming up, the flow of inspiration from your spirit will be cut off, rather like when clouds block the Sun, and then none of you can benefit. These obscured energies, become like a cage around you. You are caught between worlds, neither spiritually motivated nor with your feet firmly on the ground.

There are many things happening outside your range of awareness that restrict your freedom of action, and not everything you would like to 'free up' in your life will be possible right now, no matter how much meditation you do or therapy you undertake.

The past life has to transform itself as well, and that is by no means assured.

You are the intermediary. You were not personally a party to the creation of this karma. The ones who did it must bear the brunt of the backlash energy coming in when life responds. They have the prime duty to resolve the issues so that you can all experience the expansion and profound sense of freedom that comes on completion.

If you mistakenly believe that it is your responsibility to address these wrongdoings personally, rather than just be a conduit for their release, then you will become far more involved than you need to be. And if the past consciousness is unable to fully deal with the issues, you will be seriously affected by the build up of toxic energy between you, and you may well begin to repeat the past. In so many ways, it is largely out of your hands, but your acceptance and understanding will certainly help.

When the imbalance becomes serious, more power needs to flow in from the source to rectify this, or a period of lowered vitality or ill health will occur. You both need to progress on your respective levels by expanding towards the light as part of the shared evolutionary process and to the dark, equally. Take this into your meditation at such times to help you realise that it is only the physical you that will be subdued. The treatment then for a depleted mind or body has to encourage expansion and release on the more subtle levels.

It is not just past lives that can upset your inner composure. You are constantly being influenced subliminally by others in the spirit world you have agreed to help, and this includes some from your ancestral line, your parents and right back for seven generations. They can reach you through the genes and, more usually, when they approach in their astral bodies. These folk can be quite insistent, particularly when they believe they have failed you in some way and are determined to put it right.

Not all of them will find it easy to work in harmony with you, and this may make you irritable and despondent at times. Knowing this, you can learn to deal with it, because you are no stranger to these conditions. Your ability to accommodate multiple influences has been built up over many lives, but now some of the coping mechanisms you use have become ineffective.

Each life is geared to extending its soul capabilities and it is quite a mammoth task these days to assimilate the plethora of energies bombarding you all. In order to reach a destination beyond your present limits, the strands of your life need to be meticulously simplified; but sometimes one life tries to break away, wants to be a free spirit. Don't you sometimes wish you could do this—get away from it all? But, in the process, the continuing integration of all the lives is undermined and the distant connection you have with your source self is weakened. But fortunately the process is fully supported on the levels above by guides and guardians and loved ones provided you are willing to open up to their influence.

In the crucial early days of a life, the sense that there is unity in all things will not have been entirely lost. When a spiritual path is begun later on, the yin and the yang, which have developed in the meantime as forces of opposition, must become paragons of co-operation once again, together reaching out beyond the confines of the sense mind to spiritualize the unfolding human nature.

If you seem totally stuck, then these two principles may be at loggerheads. An emphasis somewhere needs to be reversed or the region where they overlap may have to be adjusted. If you have been meditating in your head, try reaching into your heart to contact the Christ power. That will enable the spirit to influence the soul more effectively, which can then in its turn relay a greater understanding of your divine purpose into your conscious mind. From there, this can be extended into more inclusive forms of expression, where before it was ghettoised.

This will enable the divine part to slip through the cracks in your defences, fleetingly at first but, with discipline, the spiritual and the human will be experienced as both separate and unified at the same time. Then the inner intelligence will be able to find ways through to assert its authority over your life.

Even if you engage in meditation, or participate in one of the many courses of self discovery available today, or you have a creative gift that fulfils you, there are times where all inner contact with a divine presence seems to desert you. This is when the soul is at its most elevated, and therefore, most distant. It is important to welcome these periods when they come, even though they may remind you of the time as a child when the inner worlds were cut off from you, and the pain is even more intense now. It requires true faith in the essential goodness of life to be revived so that the divine connection can be reinforced and sustained despite the fact that life does not appear to be supporting it.

**The New Children**
The souls coming fresh into the world at this time have bodies rather different from ours. They are finer, more porous to the rays of spirit; they are exhibiting a more ethereal quality.

The splitting of the atom, with its special kind of radiation, has provided the energy needed to refine the composition of matter, and the opening up of the ozone layer has allowed intense rays of light to beat down into the Earth's atmosphere, to be absorbed by all living things, and to transform the way new life is created.

This is a culmination in the long process of refinement in the Earth's journey of discovery which we humans share, when the rapidly quickening energies of transition and transmutation will be able to take over.

Evolved souls adjust well into these more subtle bodies, but less mature souls often resist and rebel because their level of evolution is not in tune with the new vibrations. Also, the former lives coming around them are not able to provide the kind of support they need. To relate to the world, unfolding so rapidly now, requires a soul flexibility that many of them do not have. They are encouraging a life that reflects their old concerns and aspirations based in the Piscean ways of exclusivity, divisiveness, and greed.

They are merely tinkering with their past errors of judgment rather than opening up to the subtle sensitivities of the Aquarian nature that lie beyond them. They did not need to experience anything like this when they were on Earth, and they cannot understand the completely different kind of existence that is unfolding, the dramatic changes needed in the coming decades.

The very sensitive children will find that their parents' generation will not understand and nurture the new qualities waiting to emerge from within them, so the first wave of truly Aquarian souls will probably be misunderstood, and perhaps punished for their differences. They will not wish to fit into the established structures and mores of society, nor should they, but many of them cannot express a generosity of spirit yet and are becoming far too isolated. But, as this kind of etherealization becomes more established, these youngsters will discover effective ways to express their new gifts, and will develop the stamina to withstand the severe social confusion that will continue to rage around them over many years to come. Such divisive karma is of the past, and they will be demanding a fresh start.

**Gifts of the Spirit**
The purpose of all human existence requires every individual life form to extend its existing soul qualities and, at the same time, learn through experience what life in its manifest abundance is really asking of them and how to negotiate it successfully.

You might not always be aware of why you're doing certain things; you just feel motivated in that direction. Youngsters go out on their skateboards to have fun, yet they are also training their physical reflexes to manoeuvre and, in the process, they develop confidence. If you are going to do anything well, you must have a natural aptitude brought forward from past experience. The balance and basic finesse that these kids exhibit, was there when they were born, but this must be developed into a mature skill. Perhaps, they are involved in an early phase of some ability that will become more prominent later on, such as to be an expert ice skater.

Children love to play computer games where they try to destroy the enemy; and, of course, behind this play is a fighting instinct, a killing instinct even, that resides with a former life. In this way, it can be released without causing harm. At the same time, quick reflexes are being honed and the ability to not be caught unawares.

These children are learning skills, yet they may have absolutely no idea where this dexterity will lead them.

Sometimes, people with no previous training discover that they can do some things spontaneously. They have a natural ability which they have developed in the past, and the life that was responsible is still there, so the talent can grow in both of them.

Let us suppose that musical expertise was developed in a former life. In the spirit world, it has been taken a step forward, and this progress needs to be tested in a new life where the challenges are different. The former personality was a popular composer in 1743, but to create that music now would provide no progress. The present life needs to tune into that earlier life, because there is no point in starting from scratch. What was achieved before is then modified, brought up to date, perhaps even rebelled against; but, that is the starting point.

**The Career**
Let us imagine that you intend to create opera, realising that much that is composed today is discordant, reflecting the times. You want to do better than that. You aspire to a new level of harmony in music, but obstructions from the past are getting in the way and you seem to be making no headway. You will need great patience to avoid feeling frustrated creatively. You want success and the rewards that accompany it, but an old lazy streak has been aroused in you. You don't always put in the hours needed to hone your gifts properly.

Perhaps music is not your thing, but you do have an artistic flair that you would like to put to good use. You have an astute business acumen, and an accompanying ability to work well with others, so you could be successful in media marketing. But the corporate world isn't to your liking—much too ruthless and money oriented. Later, you pick up a stomach bug in Egypt and a local herbalist effects a cure. This is the clue that leads you towards a career in holistic medicine.

You might have to look far back to discover a strong reason to devote your whole life to working in this field. Perhaps it was a death at the hands of an orthodox medical practitioner in the days when medical science was rather crude and hygiene non-existent. But, in fact, you were actually one of those ignorant doctors and many people died in your hands.

So, you need to find a more holistic way of approaching an unhealthy body in this life, but which therapy? Herbalism doesn't feel right, but what about osteopathy or energy healing? There are so many choices. When your destiny was programmed into the soul, the exact form of therapy was not specified; this is one of the details that were left to be intuited later on.

The various parts of the body are linked by energy lines, and that fascinates you. So, you narrow the choice to reflexology and acupuncture. Both require a sensitive appreciation of the energies that flow and connect up different parts of the body. In acupuncture, you will put aside the intellect and develop the intuition required to precisely pin-point the spot where new vitality is needed. It also requires an intuitive understanding of how the subtle bodies interact with the physical.

Many conditions have developed due to organs or glands malfunctioning and, in reflexology, these are stimulated through specific areas of the feet which relate to them. Your choice of therapy needs to enhance the skills and attributes brought forward from other lives, and engage those areas neglected in the past. Everything in life must help the soul progress, must bring the entire human nature into synthesis and alignment.

Perhaps, the more recent lives did not develop with their feet firmly on the ground. Shoes are one way that modern man has separated himself from the earth. How marvellous it is to run on a beach, bare-footed, with the sea and the sky and the breezes liberating you from the cares of life. Many people today walk with their heads too much up in the air, preoccupied with things of the mind instead of the 'moment' as it is being experienced through the body. And so, you realise that reflexology is the therapy that best suits you and not acupuncture, which is more rarefied.

## Ways of Service

Many people are starting to understand their past as more than just a background influence, and they are learning how to focus inwardly to such an extent that the energies from those of their previous lives, wishing to transcend their limitations, can be consciously and precisely focussed into the current life without wavering. Thus, the restrictions fall away and the energies are converted into something far more substantial for you both, and later your subtle creative gifts can be engaged and directed into a form of service where a profoundly compassionate heart is linked to many others in a common cause.

How exciting it is to plunge deeper and deeper into the Earth and emerge each time triumphant. How wonderful to then take in the nourishing rays of the spiritual Sun, and burst forth as a flower of such delicacy, such beauty, that the shadow cannot exist in its vicinity.

All of us, even the lowly, the most depraved, have recently been experiencing an influx of enhanced energies into our higher bodies. And this is engaging the prayers and support of many faithful souls from over the ages, striving to make us powerful conduits for the urgent and much needed transition of the planet into a far more subtle reality.

This current influx of transformative energy, gradually working its way down through human channels, is harking back to an awakening long ago when a man of great spiritual stature came among us to demonstrate an expanded consciousness as an immediate, ongoing reality. Alas, the images he evoked of a perfect world caused fear to arise in many hearts, because the heaven on Earth that he foreshadowed was unattainable within the desire realm. It was inevitable that his true heritage would be abused and abandoned, ripped to shreds, sucked dry of its vital juices when most of us retreated from it, as he knew we would.

The churches and the common moral codes encouraged this fear by displacing and venerating this perfection and we cast many of the natural human impulses into the pit of shame. We did not know that, in isolating and rejecting our strong and potentially destructive urges, we were, in fact, empowering them. Only now can these base human drives be acknowledged without guilt and without trepidation, thereby, liberating the soul in new and exciting ways for the betterment of the Great Spirit that makes the true life possible.

Those who feel that they share a responsibility for the degradation of this magnificent creation must be willing to do something about it. They must liberate all levels of dark and light within themselves by merging the yin and yang and by bringing the past and future together in the absolutely perfect present. To do this is to release the divine potential, is to arouse from within the maelstrom of karma engulfing the planet at this time, a renewed passion for the noble life.

# 8
# Karma Explored

People tend to think of past lives in the context they were lived. You are told that you had a life in Judea two thousand years ago, and it's very appealing isn't it, to imagine that, but this is not a useful reality to concentrate on now. Past lives are only past in the sense that resonances from those lives, as they were lived, remain active and these trigger off memories. All of your former lives have developed since. You may not be able to see this, but some of them are relating with you in this time we call 'now'. They are actually present lives functioning on a different plane.

When you pass to the spirit world and ascend to the level of your soul evolution, you must leave behind the energies specific to the life you recently lived in order to progress further, returning to them only when you need to re-engage the physical experience. Then the old feelings return, along with the urge to continue with that life in some way; but, of course, the world has moved on. Any unresolved matters will have to be adapted to a new environment.

When, in a later incarnation, it is necessary to meet up again with those you harmed, they too will have progressed, though not necessarily to the same degree. The disharmony will remain but the unfamiliar conditions will be used to completely refine the ways of relating in order to move beyond it.

**What is Karma?**
The word karma may cause you to think of torture and killing, the terrible acts that provide the daily papers with their sensational content, but karma is essentially any slight imbalance in the human dynamic that is sustained. In its simplest form, it probably wouldn't be noticed. It is the residue of incomplete experience in the normal course of life, anything not fully resolved at the time.

Where further imbalances are added, a severely distorted energy will be built up, precipitating a much more convoluted and precarious situation later on.

Of course, to have equality there must be positive karma also—anything affirmative and loving that was not responded to on the physical level at the time. From these secret thoughts and simple acts of kindness, a store of vital energy is built up in the ethers close to you.

Expressions of goodwill by any devoted group contribute life-enhancing energies into much larger repositories of beneficial thought which are seen by some psychics as clouds with a scintillating pure white sheen and, if human evolution is to proceed, these must exceed any retrogressive build-up, which is a black and ominous thunderstorm of a cloud. The largest of these collective banks are linked to progressive initiatives world-wide, and can be drawn on at a time of serious need.

It is not so much that karma is a debt needing to be repaid, but rather, it is a displacement needing to be re-aligned. Where one or more of the balances within us are out of kilter, polarised in any direction, including being skewed towards either the inner or outer reality, it requires a very firm energy adjustment to get the various destiny strands into a focussed and fully integrated progression.

Any form of imbalance that is retained can be regarded as karma, and because imbalance is an integral part of the way things happen in our world, life itself is, in a sense, karma. In its purest, most natural form, human experience requires a constant moving away and moving back into balance, not unlike breathing in and having to breathe out. However, when the out breathe does not fully expel, tension builds up in the body. That is a sure sign of karma. You can see from this example, that a complete outworking is a mammoth task when there are many former lives involved.

In their early lives, people tend to choose situations that allow them a great deal of simple harmony. They do not venture out much into the unknown. A few of their group, with spiritual ambition alive in their hearts, will take responsibility to heal the contentious situations that arise in their community. In the process, they will learn how to extend a congenial attitude into an ever-widening sphere of influence. These are the ones who move the purpose of the spirit family forward by taking on leadership roles effectively. Whether you realise it or not, you are here as an act of service to your affinity group and the planet; all of us are. And, at times, this requires us to tread a very exacting path.

When monks and spiritual teachers from the East come into the harsher environments in the West, they are outside the comfortable embrace of their traditional support network. All too often, they are completely baffled by the range and intensity of temptation and cannot cope. Quite a few teachers of yoga who went to America were drummed out of the organisations they founded due to sexual indiscretion. Spiritual progress is achieved by moving step-by-step into more complex situations while retaining balance there.

**Personal Karma**
A great deal of karma is created between just two people, very often in the immediate family. Many persistent behaviour patterns develop within family relationships—distorted tendencies dragged to the surface from past lives that lead, in their repetition, to a rigidity of mind and heart, or a life of excess. However, it doesn't matter what restrictions you have, or what compulsive behaviour you may display, gratitude for your many blessings is the way out of them.

As an example: a brother who stole from you in a former life has joined your circle of friends. You can't seem to contain the envious thoughts that keep arising because he has more money than you and his material life flows more smoothly that yours does and, worst of all, he seems to be more popular in social situations. You may not exactly want to take what is his, a direct retaliation, but when you have the opportunity to offer him financial assistance, you just don't bother.

On many occasions you'll get little opportunities to overcome the inherited resentment from that former life and for both of you to exercise a generosity of spirit towards each other. The full resolution requires a genuine coming together in mutual respect and co-operation that leaves you both in a better position than before.

Karma is a natural consequence of living in a dualistic world. It is being built up all the time, both the positive and the negative varieties: a kind thought or a warm smile towards someone, who doesn't see it, is used to cultivate a compassionate heart. A surge of anger, not properly released, which continues to seethe away in the background, builds up a dangerous resentment that destroys a close friendship. It is felt in the tension that you hold in your shoulders; or in a sleepless night where you toss and turn and cannot find peace; or it gets in the way of clear sight in some situation that results in a missed opportunity.

Go further out of balance and you increase the karmic build-up to where it completely suppresses the drive to fulfil your destiny in some way. It is not a matter of your actions or behaviour being good or bad, either life spurs you on to fulfil your dreams or a mesh of frustration builds up instead. Disharmony transformed by a buoyant mind gets the creative juices flowing and the link to the spirit is gradually strengthened. Then you become more accomplished at negotiating life's pathway and feeling good about yourself as you do.

It is all a learning experience and each attempt made to bring yourself into a serene frame of mind must, in the long-term, lead to a more mature approach to life and stable relationships. However, every time you aggravate some distressing area and do not deal with it, you encase yourself in a mental cage that grows, and breaking free will become increasingly difficult. But even if you have chosen a tortuous path, by continuing to strive for clarity, you will eventually learn the lessons embedded in this self-induced aggravation, and they will have been comprehensively learned.

Another view of personal karma sees it as an accumulation of all that has come forward in your life in response to energies released from your destiny pattern that have not yet been effectively integrated into your journey—all that is not at peace with the present. Mistakes of the past that have had lasting consequences, that remain active and invasive, could be described as chronic karma; but sometimes you let old patterns of behaviour and belief remain unnecessarily. You have done what was required to resolve some difficult situation, you should be basking in your success, but entrenched beliefs of unworthiness and shame are difficult to budge. Confined to the deeper recesses of your being, they constantly retard progress.

Nothing is more damaging than to hold these things in and to let them fester, for once out in the open, they will be seen as largely without foundation and the detrimental effects will vanish. People are very often their own harshest critics. It is important to realise that the Divine judge is much more forgiving than the hell-fire Christians wish us to believe, for you are, in the last analysis, your own judge and jury. Indeed, the ravages of guilt can be far more karmically damaging than the original act.

**Addictions**

Remember that previous lives seeking some kind of resolution through the current incarnation are there, close by, hoping to influence events for the better, but very often, if they have an addictive nature, it is a vicarious pleasure they end up promoting. Compulsive energy patterns from the past, once re-introduced, will inevitably unbalance the present life, and the urge to act them out again becomes compelling.

Let us consider the situation where a man has a former life in the background who was an alcoholic. He has recently lost his job and pressures are building up in a love relationship, so he drinks too much and too often. And whenever he goes into a bar, the past life is likely to be there with him.

The sensible thing would be for the past personality to approach just a little at a time, so that the craving doesn't escalate. "No, I don't need another," he says, and his companions jeer at him when he persists. Each time temptation is overcome, the strength to resist is built up in the soul. Then the former alcoholic comes a little closer. It is an ongoing process.

Both lives, present and past, have to strengthen their resolve, but where the earlier life has been drawn too close, too early, the incarnate one will feel inadequate, overwhelmed. To bolster his self-esteem, he will try to justify his actions and hide the extent of his cravings from his family, those who care the most, and from his employers. The downward spiral is well under way.

Together, the two lives must progressively develop the strength of will to remain in control. For a time it will be a balancing act. Everyone around will be offering "just one more". They don't like it when one of their group is showing more resolve than they are, and they will intensify their efforts to keep their friend down to their level.

Addictions tend to prevent spiritual expansion by blocking the energy flow that will bring greater understanding and resolve with it. The hedonistic lifestyle has its attractions but, gradually, the past personality releases the addictive tendency through the growing will power of the present one. To support this process, other past lives are drawn in close, lives that had successfully developed self-discipline in some area, and their stabilising influence helps the incarnate person to overcome the craving.

What is achieved on one level is not automatically relayed to another. The Earth atmosphere retains a memory of that earlier life and this can also re-enforce the old tendencies. Even when addictions to substances or obsessive behaviour have been dealt with on the astral level by drawing down the necessary resolve from levels above, the rebalanced energies still need to be sent plummeting into the earth so that the human aspect of the condition can be dispersed. Until that happens, alcoholism remains a definite possibility.

All forms of desire unbalance, and this is complicated when two past lives with the same issue are there behind the scenes. Two alcoholics and a potential one on the Earth. The addiction had become entrenched by the end of the second life and so, this is going to be a tricky situation to resolve. Obviously, if they both moved in close to the new life together, it would be a foregone conclusion.

There's no point in attempting any karmic outworking until both former lives have done enough work on themselves in the spirit world and exposed the nuances of the dark energy that they had been unable to reconcile when the latter of the two was incarnate.

In order to deal with the issue, the cause has to be fully addressed, and though this lies with the earliest life, it is usually the one that has done the most inner work and has the greater strength of purpose, who will be the first to come forward. It needs great sensitivity to know what the human participant can handle, to know just which former life should take the lead, to what extent, and when.

If they had probed more deeply in the Hall of Incarnations, they would have seen how the first of these past lives fell into this way of behaviour, and why it was sustained in the second. When understanding is on the surface, over-optimism can easily lead to a belief that the issue will be more easily dealt with than is likely. The present life will suffer for any such miscalculation. However, it could be, that whatever they attempt, the problem is too deeply ingrained for a simple resolution. These impacted energies are often caused by a repeated dampening down of inner pain following a loss or following a failure, with despair and a deep sense of loneliness overwhelming every situation. Alcohol replaces this with a freedom that forgets. It is a false freedom but, for a time, the pain is put aside.

Some people drink to release their inhibitions and let out some suppressed feelings, usually anger, and abusive behaviour is unleashed. When the alcohol loses its effect, some are overwhelmed by remorse, but this indulgence will do little to change their behaviour.

**An Addiction Persists**
Let us look at a life in Bavaria in the sixteenth century when a man had fallen out of love for his wife and had inflicted a great deal of casual violence onto her. All his affection was for their young daughter. He felt that he had been given the responsibility to love and protect this beautiful soul, but his wife could no longer stand his abusive ways and attempted to escape to a distant village taking the daughter with her. Alas, they were killed in an accident on a mountain pass. This man could not be consoled and he turned to what he saw as the only way out, to drink.

That is clear enough but, in a later life which was again male, there was a tendency for him to drink as part of the camaraderie of the group of farmers who met regularly in a North of England hostelry to let off steam after a hard day's toil in the fields but only occasionally to excess. This was in the mid-eighteenth century. He loved his wife deeply, but she had married a little beneath her station, and had become tired of the drudgery of the farming life. She remembered the exciting times when her father, a member of a local mill owning family, had taken her to the large city nearby. There she had danced and was courted by influential men from the area. The life she was now leading and the somewhat boorish nature of her husband caused her to think of those better times and she occasionally found an excuse to go to Bradford with her brother to celebrate with some old friends. But these women were not serious types; they indulged in the good life with all its trivia and tattle.

She did not tell her husband about these visits or of her dissatisfaction with her life in the village, and he continued to love her. Her visits to Bradford increased but, in between, she accepted her lot. At no point did she feel the need to be unfaithful. However, the husband found out about the clandestine visits when a neighbouring farmer saw her there. So, the next time she journeyed with her brother to the city, he followed them. In a drunken rage, he killed the brother. He was tried, convicted and put in prison, where he blamed the brother for leading her astray. He never lost his love for her and was shocked to learn that she had eventually passed. After his release, he took up heavy drinking and died of it.

The daughter he loved in the Bavarian life was his wife in this, and his Bavarian wife was now her brother. Quite a complex continuation of the earlier situation in which the loves and enmities, the loss and the sense of betrayal had resurfaced. Now, moving forward to a later life where many of the same ingredients were re-visited.

Of course, there had been other incarnations since the English one but, in these lives, the addiction issue was left to one side. (Such things are only dealt with when compensatory qualities have been established which will be needed to overcome that weakness.) So, as an artist, a sensitivity was honed; in a business life, there was a strong determination to succeed; and in a mining family, where toxic fumes shortened the life of his father, he decided to pursue another way of life. Other developmental work was done in the spirit world to counteract a tendency to self harm, and some progress was made in the matter of loyalty. But now it was time to resolve the addiction once and for all and to test other former tendencies such as impulsiveness and resentment. The life for this was chosen to be in France during the Second World War.

Here the Bavarian wife, who was also the brother in England, is this time, a brother who becomes heavily involved in the resistance movement. Our man became an informer, a perverse form of loyalty, and this resulted in the brother being captured by the Germans along with other members of that group which included the daughter he had loved in Bavaria. Later, he was ostracised by his community when the truth came out. He was plunged into a deep depression, relieved only by drink. After many years he was able to overcome this compulsion, but he remained a troubled man. The main reason for this, was that he had harmed the one he loved most without realising it—but the past lives knew and their pain was transmitted down to him right through to the end of his life.

This detailed progression of lives has been presented so you can understand the ways in which these issues of karma repeat themselves and become ingrained. Many people today have returned to unravel very complicated entanglements of this kind; that have tightened their grip on the inner self with a whole complex of conflicting attitudes, impulses, fears and allegiances.

In such cases, you might think that the Lords of Karma would have a difficult job to do, but from their elevated position, they can easily configure a life out of the various ingredients in much the same way that your cosmologists delve deeply into the mysteries of the Universe when most people remain bewildered. Such an overview becomes possible when evolution allows it, just as later on, we will all enjoy a much greater receptivity to the thoughts and intentions of the creator.

# 9
# Soul Qualities

**Perseverance**

In lifetime after lifetime, some people just don't achieve the degree of spiritual awakening they are hoping for. The same old issues constantly defeat them. Even though grace had been granted following the previous life, when the failures and disappointments were put aside, the pressure within the source self became so intense, so insistent, that a new soul was virtually impelled down to Earth; and here it is now in a new body, learning its lessons the hard way, frustrated at every turn.

Perseverance is a most important quality needed in every life. However, where people become goal orientated, where their wish to be validated and rewarded for their effort becomes paramount, perseverance will be counter-productive. Having a destination is useful and there is no harm in being praised, but a soul tension develops if a person cannot do without. It is vital to do things for their own sake, relying on a simple pride in the smallest achievement to keep one going. Though, once on a spiritual path, life will usually test that to the limit.

A writer I know, set out to craft a ground-breaking first novel to launch her career, but her book was rejected and she reacted to this by deciding that perhaps this is not what she really should be doing. So, she went on to something else.

People rarely land upon the world stage as overnight successes. Most have undertaken a long apprenticeship before that, unrecognised—if not in this life, then in a previous one. Without this, they would get early recognition and then slip back later on, unable to keep the creative momentum going, set in the same old grooves, singing the same old songs, teaching the same old ideas, because they do not understand that spiritual progress lies in renewal.

**When Inertia Prevails**

The opposite of perseverance is indolence or laziness. A person who has no ambition in life, who just can't be bothered, may actually have a very strong ambition that has become totally impacted, though this is not always the case.

Let us consider a female Chinese incarnation who lived a privileged life in a household with many servants. She only put in effort if she felt like it. This was not the first time she had incarnated into a well-to-do family, indeed she usually avoided those of low status. Pride in her superior worth had become ingrained in her.

At the suggestion of the Lords of Karma, the following male soul incarnated into an impoverished, though titled family, determined to be an even more successful businessman than his grandfather had been. His charm, and a slick way with words, convinced some financiers to back him in a business venture. But there was an overconfidence stemming from these earlier privileged lives. He felt it would all just fall into place and so he went ahead without the necessary planning and promotion. The venture failed and the backers withdrew their support. He pleaded with his friends to give him another chance, but they knew he lacked the necessary business acumen and wisely refused.

He couldn't understand the failure, blaming it on the 'stupid people' who did not see the value in his enterprise. He had been brought down a peg, and in that life, a great frustration built up. Eventually, he felt that, no matter what he did, he would not succeed, there was no point in even trying. So, there are now two lives in the background, one privileged, one fallen on hard times, both with a strong, but frustrated, sense of god-given importance.

Progressing forward to a current male life, there are no servants, but his wife, the aspiring novelist I referred to earlier, is happy enough to do most of the chores. She is working as an editorial assistant in a small publishing company. Her husband, after a not too successful career in T.V. production, has been made redundant; and he has fallen into the old patterns of dependency and lack of motivation, content to let someone else do the things he could well do for himself.

Already, there is a tremendous gap between what he came to achieve and what is actually happening. Then, his wife loses her job when the company folds and, in the ensuing fight for survival, he feels pulled apart, bewildered, angry, betrayed. Behind the scenes, the earlier life who did not have to fight for anything and the one with an entrenched sense of failure are trying to arouse sufficient determination from their own energy banks built up since they were incarnate but, because of the lack of effort put in by the one on Earth, it is held back; they cannot access it.

The former urgency in the destiny emanations has weakened and so, all the favourable opportunities attracted to him remain out of sight and out of reach. There is little activity anywhere. The man hopes that his wife will get the success as a writer she deserves, letting him off the hook, but this doesn't happen. She has karma that complements his own. In other relationships, the patterns may be different; one moves on while the other does not. But here they are both stuck.

Life can only meet them halfway. So, they must go on without becoming bitter or defeatist, gradually arousing a greater sense of purpose and reaching out from it. An obvious way out of their dilemma is to take employment they feel is beneath them, allowing a new evolutionary impulse to come up from the Earth to meet the inspiration from above. The primary attraction is the source self, and progress is determined by how effectively it can stimulate a momentum into the far reaches of itself.

The previous lives have worked hard in the afterlife to establish self motivation, for that quality is essential there, and the present male life will need to instinctively reach up to access this when the old obstructive energies are re-activated and rise up to challenge any efforts he makes to establish a niche in this highly competitive media field.

Where there is not the will power, the strength of purpose necessary to counteract this lethargy that stems from earlier rejections and failures, it is likely that the former life is struggling as well. Even if one is holding the other back, it is a joint responsibility, both need to focus intently within so that the source power can flow through them strongly enough to reach the Earth.

Our man believes his wife is letting him down and decides to leave her. Somehow this unblocks her route to literary recognition. You can see why so many struggle for recognition in the cut-throat literary world. It is not just a matter of talent. Her book sold well and so, that part of the destiny pattern was completed. The past and present lives shared the benefits in their own ways and then, in came another past life with something new to work on, and the journey continued.

"Is there no end to it?", you might reasonably be thinking; the answer, of course, is "Definitely not!" However, in the future, you may be able to handle any new challenges and the resistance to them with more equanimity, but whether they will be easier to negotiate is entirely dependent on the amount of karma you've taken on in this incarnation.

**Refining the qualities**
The Buddhist faith is very effective in building up qualities that lead to an integrated consciousness. Their teachings stress mindfulness and respect for all sentient beings, and they encourage seekers to look carefully at their self-destructive attitudes and behaviour so that they can winkle out any insidious mental deceptions hiding there. This is a good thing, but it does not go far enough. As you progress, your life involves matters of increasing subtlety that are very personal to you. Refining the qualities is essential if you are to negotiate life in ways that are not rooted in the old desire patterns, for this cannot be achieved by merely extending goodness on the human level. You have to raise consciousness, not merely expand it.

No capability or understanding is automatically transferred from one level to another, you must reach up to it to the same degree that it reaches down to you, and down to it as it reaches up to you, otherwise you just won't be stable enough to fully engage an opportunity when it comes. You access higher abilities only when Earth meets up with heaven in your heart.

Your individual destiny pattern is layered into your etheric consciousness, with each gradation having a finer vibration. This enables human life to unfold in an orderly sequence. Very few intended events are time specific, but there are occasions when a repeat energy pattern needs to be activated at exactly the same time as in a former life. Most destined phases are set into motion only when a previous one has been completed.

When a new initiative is activated, karmic energies may immediately surround it, denying it the freshness and simplicity you would expect. On other occasions, preparatory work may have to done before the karma reveals itself. This is important, for if the whole of a particular karmic energy were to be aroused at the one time, you would be battling to cope.

### Early lives underpin the present

Most formative existences were experienced in a bubble of child-like innocence in quite primitive situations where communities were naturally supportive, relationships were developed simply and the joy of love flowed. This early harmony was necessary, so that a sensitive attunement to the elements and nature would be built up to underpin later lives. Clearly, today, this connection has been lost.

In so many people, a great disassociation between the spirit and the soul is being reflected into a society that has ceased providing a passage between the God father and the Earth mother, and individuals are feeling totally cut off from their source of power when karma rises up unexpectedly.

A woman who has been accepting of her husband going out with his friends, leaving her alone with the baby, suddenly feels abandoned. Out of the blue, a sudden shift, and resentment rises from out of it and grows. This has come forward from another life altogether. And then, an opportunity for adultery appears for the husband, which is also a repeat event from a former existence. She finds out about it and is faced with a crucial dilemma.

The energy of genuine love and trust built up by this couple in an early life needs to be brought in to transform the indiscretions being acted out now. Nothing positive is ever wasted. If you should work harder than you need for a good cause, or walk that extra mile to visit a sick friend, or display kindness that cannot be accepted at the time, these simple acts build up vibrant supportive energies around your soul that can be harnessed later when you are in need.

While you are indeed the sum total of everything you have ever thought and done, and that will remain with you throughout eternity, the ability to externalise this is appropriately challenged as the source self matures.

Most people, oblivious to the past elements, are caught unawares when a difficult karmic situation arises. Had she approached a medium at the beginning of the friendship, she might have been told, "I see a wonderful relationship ahead. You are going to be so happy, my dear." If it had been "Oh, it might seem to be the right partner for you, but watch out, there are nasty things on the horizon. I caution you to be careful, my dear," that would not have been helpful. She would have spent her time trying to avoid the difficulties rather than just living the life immediately before her.

The various phases of the destiny pattern are only activated when outer circumstances allow it, and the ability to register possible future events must necessarily be limited. Only the advanced ones can see deeply into another person's soul and they would always transmit this knowledge wisely. The critical elements in your life are inactive until their moment arrives, and then the support and understanding that comes from spirit can help you through it.

Now, put yourself into another hypothetical situation. You have gone into a business venture with three friends. There is camaraderie and optimism there, for the karma that you incurred together is not yet pressing in on you. An intuitive impression, picked up early on, indicated that you were fellow prospectors in the Australian gold rush. "Good," you thought, "we are going to strike gold in our venture," and you pressed on. However, the next phase of the past has started to arise, where greed took over and you fell out, and one of you even died as a result.

So, here you are, partners again, and you are being offered opportunities that are not entirely above board. There are disagreements, because two of your partners have done less work on moral issues since that life than you have. Conflict arises when an underhand move is proposed that might force the most ethical member of your group out; he would lose everything. Loyalty, now, becomes an issue.

You can see how the past shapes the future. That is karma in a nutshell. And when you take these personal situations into the wider arena, the primitive loyalties that were polarised into factions, with class or economic divisions ruthlessly maintained, the haves and the have nots perpetually held in their place, it is obvious that, in many people, the early harmonies have morphed into a pathological disregard for those who do not share their limited mental outlook and way of life.

When people come together in later lives, they bring with them all sorts of complex issues and attitudes collected along the way that prevent them from effectively relating and truly caring. You only have to look at the power games that go on in any government today to see what happens when the spirit family members are drawing on all sorts of blind allegiances and unproductive alliances from former times, without knowing how to effectively replace them.

**The Past Points the Way**
Some of your incarnations were ahead of their time. There was no acceptance for your ideas and abilities possible. You felt ignored, under-valued, put down. Yet, provided you did not indulge in resentment, good karma would have been built up through your efforts to achieve. Some creative people go through life without any recognition whatsoever, and are immensely surprised when they graduate to the higher realms to find that their works of art have brought much joy to those on that level. Everything expressed, that is beautiful and divinely inspired, resonates on more than one plane.

The Master Jesus demonstrated this when he placed a great accumulation of concentrated energy in the ethers at the time leading up to his death. It is only now that the more progressive members of our world are beginning to access this on a wide scale. Any acts, selflessly executed and not responded to at the time, can continue to have ramifications and provide opportunities far into the future. Many deeds of the true Masters, resonating through to assist us today, are perfect examples of evolution delayed.

In nature, some animals store up more than they presently require. They understand, from the past experience of the species, that at some future time there may be the need. There surely have been times when you have come in contact with someone you think has nothing in common with you, just not your sort of person. Yet, some assistance flows to you quite unexpectedly. That may well be beneficent karma coming in from a previous life together.

Many things from the past are biding their time for the right moment to intervene and bring opportunity or resolution to a particular situation. Something developed well beyond the needs of that earlier incarnation may soon come in to give you a boost when your resolve is flagging and, very often, the aid comes from the one that was helped in a former time. But, sometimes it just flows in from the storehouse of energy that has been built up, and uses a stranger as the way to assist you.

Now, imagine a life as an artist where recognition did not come. It was necessary merely to discover the essence of creativity. The eyes needed to see the divine perfection in all things, the heart needed to channel into those works of art the profound truth that beyond all human suffering lies the compassion of the ages, and the mind needed to express the eternal nature of the liberated imagination, for that is the beginning of true artistry.

When faced by a blank canvas, trust knew that everything needing expression would be there as its moment arose. The many flashes of inspiration, those brief insights into the deeper purpose of life, were built on through faith, and then inexhaustible streams of awakened consciousness began to flow through into the paintings. It was enough that the spirit had taken charge so that the purity would manifest, and the deceptive forces would finally meet their match.

Courage had been aroused to step into the creative unknown,

where the fleeting nature of true opportunity must be ridden like a wave, not grasped, and diminished. First, simple acceptance needed to be there, then trust and faith, and each was discovered in their turn, the three prime aspects of that great, supreme quality, patience.

How difficult patience is for the unruly earth mind, to see things as they really are, to accept that none of us are, ultimately, the instigator of anything. Trust is a deeply humbling position to set out from. To step forward, powered only by faith, requires one to put aside the past and the future, and surrender to a higher purpose in the present, even when your knees are shaking with fear, even when others are ranged against you, and you feel terribly alone.

The elevated states of consciousness, when they are reached, are merely refinements of earlier achievements, for these spiral around and return regularly as gifts to implement and balance on higher levels of expertise. Jesus is seen by many as the epitome of Masterhood, a man who could balance a profound degree of both the dark and the light and express this through simple acts of unconditional love.

The qualities of perseverance, persistence, tenacity, are all traits that could just as easily become the stock in trade of the bully. The balancing feminine qualities must accompany them.

Jesus performed many healing miracles, yet it was the more sensational ones that generated a buzz in the masses. He was an occultist, certainly, but he rarely used those gifts publicly. His reputation for miraculous acts was largely built on hearsay.

Masters usually appear to be like anyone else, but the profound qualities they demonstrate are sure to include flexibility, the ability to never get fixated on any outcome. Masters intuitively know when to act. They have no allegiances other than to truth. They step forward and life unfolds before them as they know it will. They don't bother to attempt anything that they sense will not be accepted. They are not preparing for a successful moment, they are living it.

When you cultivate the gift of clear sight, you won't waste time on fruitless endeavour, bashing your head against endless brick walls. Early frustrations are the signals that a slight adjustment is required to nip future chaos in the bud. Resolve them promptly.

The final initiations into Masterhood require adepts to step into the limelight, publicly and courageously demonstrating profound abilities at a critical moment in human history, to walk in the light of a great avatar that preceded them. Gandhi was one of these. He understood timing and he never engaged his British adversaries on their level. Like a master samurai, he waited for them to blink first. He admitted that if he had tried these tactics earlier, it would not have worked, or in another country. He knew exactly when to act to face down these particular oppressors.

There was an exceptionally angry former life with him. However, this had matured from resentment into the much more spiritually valid form, righteous anger, and Gandhi directed this with absolute precision into the injustices in his world, while deflecting away most of the resistance. He focussed within himself to such a degree that a higher power was channelled through him, transforming this anger into something much more potent. And this power was shared with those close to him, so that their collective force was unstoppable. It cut through the English defences like a laser. He instinctively knew how to balance the light and the dark, but he also had the flexibility to manoeuvre this 'laser' into exactly the right position for maximum effect. If only the British and the Americans had used similar tactics instead of invading Iraq in the way that they did.

These are vital lessons for those taking on the advanced ways of service, the ones who are close to Masterhood. How far you are able to engage in that kind of global service is dependent on past achievements for, though the mind of God is always available to you from deep within, the ability to manifest it is an evolving thing.

## The Little Things

Most karma has the habit of bursting out in a most annoying fashion just as you think you have achieved some measure of stability. At this birth of the Age of Aquarius there is an urgency to complete, and the great majority of people have returned with some of their less commendable traits to the fore. "Humanity is slipping back," people moan. "The world has become so corrupt," when, in reality, the hidden corruptions of the past are more out in the open with the underbelly exposed. But the truly good and pure is also closer to the surface, waiting for its chance to emerge rejoicing.

The mature qualities would seem to need a more favourable climate to find further expression at this time, but the power that they represent is concentrated behind the scenes and some of it is available when you reach deep enough into your heart to access it. A pioneer can only bring forward what is needed and the more profound lessons to be learnt are totally linked in with humanity's need to evolve in harmony with the planet.

The clash of sounds emanating from so many places on Earth is almost deafening today. Many people are trying to deaden their senses to a reminder of their own turbulent past. They fear being drawn into the energies of it again in this very unstable present. The clamour is an assault on those fine souls who are trying to reach further into the subtle realms to access the harmonious waves of co-operative energy now awaiting release.

The global domination by big business and the media merely reflects disharmony in the collective consciousness. They are not the cause of our malaise though their incessant invitations to succumb to their ever widening extremes of control has sapped humanity's capacity for true compassion and threatened the planet's vitality and viability. Seekers are diverted into the more glamorous ways of spiritual adventuring, but a calm inner focus is needed to bring true harmony into being. It is the overwhelming challenge of this time.

Although most people only value the strong, dramatic, breakout experiences in their life, it is the little things that provide the soul with its main source of strength, for these are cumulative in spiritual terms. Much that passes un-noticed in your life helps to mould you. Every cell is a motivating force, every smile brings out the best in you.

Some people are in your life for only a short period of time, you get something from each other and then off they go. The karma has been not repaid, exactly, because that speaks of debt and puts one of the participants in an inferior position; the word 'realigned' is better. Karma is realigned. Each such encounter brings an incomplete energy in from the past that must be balanced in the present. And that is very rewarding, because both parties feel empowered, without necessarily knowing why.

If a person who has unresolved issues with you becomes unavailable, another person, who needs that kind of help, will step in to take over. Benefit comes to both of you through this encounter, and it is likely that the one who missed out will likewise receive what is needed in a similarly displaced context and so, a reconciliatory impulse resonates down through the ethers that brings all four of the participants into a state of completion. The karma between the original couple is worked out without there having been a direct contact.

Everything in this universe is seeking balance, even if it is sometimes by circuitous routes. Denial of our karmic responsibilities so often leads to restriction and frustration where people, knowing that they have come to work out some destructive part of their history, cannot face it. The power for renewal has to be drawn out of the old ways, by transforming them in the present, and while this requires detachment, it cannot usually be completed alone.

The inharmonious tendencies have to be embraced and resolved, not hidden away, not held down or denied. Indeed, 'to seal the door where evil dwells,' is not usually the way to go. For suppressed disharmony causes it to swell in strength, till it breaks out in a more destructive way than if it had been released and dealt with a little at a time. But how do we arouse the extra resolve, the extra power to dissolve the restriction when we have not succeeded countless times before?

So many people who call themselves spiritual are reluctant to hand themselves over to the spirit within, which is surprising, for resolution comes to those who do. They know that they must put aside times for subtle reflection on a regular basis but they don't always do it. Only deep soul contact will lead them to confront the really big issues of their life in a new way. The purity that has been concealed must eventually be revealed.

### The Wild One and the Peasant

Now, let us look at one of the most common developmental progressions, the alternation of worldliness and introspection. Early on, these two were experienced in separate lives, when the elemental forces were visited in turn. The earth element may have been contacted as a farmer, the air as an influential scholar, the water as a nurturing mother and the fire as a community leader. There will inevitably be one warrior incarnation when the wild side runs riot and, after a war between neighbouring clans, he celebrates victory by raping and pillaging.

He is a young soul, and does not understand anything of the consequences that karma brings. He hasn't acquired the attributes of compassion, or of restraint. At home, he may be a decent enough father and husband, but once out of the control of the group morality, the primitive urges take over. He doesn't see the opposing forces as human at all, really. They are just 'the enemy'. Or they are ignorant natives and clearly inferior, not worthy of the respect that white people can command.

On returning to the spirit world, the full ramifications of his deeds are made clear to him when the significant events of his life and their consequences are re-lived. The perpetrator feels wretched and ashamed and so, in the next life, he decides to be a peasant farmer in an isolated community. He soon realises that if you don't treat the land well, it will not produce the crops, and if you don't treat the animals well, they will not serve you. Clearly, if another warrior life was to follow immediately, the destructive tendency would, most likely, be heightened rather than resolved. Therefore, a balancing life is planned which will keep him well away from situations that might provoke further retrogressive behaviour.

These compensating lives may still have the karmic aspect there on the periphery, as a reminder. Perhaps war raged around him as a child, too young to participate but, as he grows into his life as a farmer, the memory is there. The warrior instinct has been held in abeyance. The crops have to be tended or they will starve. In such a life, the natural world would speak to him and reveal many of its secrets.

Perhaps he is also a regular churchgoer, a 'god fearing' man, and he plays out his destined role as an integral part in the life of that community. He would have every opportunity to send out his prayers for peace to distant places where war still rages. These loving energies directed outwards will modify those impulses from the past that are held back in his own psyche. His whole life is devoted to establishing a balance to that previous wild behaviour.

In a later incarnation, the wheel turns and the fire is, once again, kindled in his soul when he incarnates into a situation of bitter conflict and turmoil, and he cannot help but be drawn into it. The warrior nature returns, but it is hoped that the life as a farmer can provide a harmonising energy, strong enough to transmute the more destructive of his combative inclinations when circumstances draw him towards an impending clash. There are now two past personalities there, the wild one and the peasant, influencing him with totally contrary impulses. A fearful struggle goes on inside him. "I am a churchgoer, a good man. I must not get involved with these reprehensible elements in my community. Even if others behave this way, I must not". These thoughts flood in.

But the leaders of this community are not interested in peace. They want to invade a neighbouring settlement, and take what is not theirs. They whip up dissent in the village and, on securing arms, they call for volunteers to join them. "You must think of the good of you village", they say, "It is disloyal to refuse" or even, "The gods are on our side". You will, of course, recognise this kind of emotional blackmail. It has been the rallying call for the perpetration of atrocities since humanity began, and it continues today. At that point, karmically, the man must choose.

There is a tug-of-war going on inside many people today, between two opposing past lives, that gives them little peace. A superior power is trying to reach into the Earth's atmosphere, yet the bulk of humanity is putting up a barrier, refusing to fully address the widespread inequalities that are demanding justice.

## The Choice is Yours

If the warlike element is suppressed, it builds in intensity and breaks out disastrously in a more damaging way later on. Conflict is raging all over the planet, stemming from wars of the past. Some governments regularly wage war on foreign shores, but even if you consider them unjustified, the buck cannot be passed where karma is concerned and, as global citizens, we are all responsible for each other and for the planet we live on. To bring harmony into the soul of Gaia, the Earth mother, we must further integrate our own dark and light elements by remaining true to our highest principles.

In business today, it is very difficult not to arouse a ruthless streak, going in for the kill in the market place, but if you always treat your colleagues well, give value for your profit, or your wage, these little things will cumulatively build up a more respectful attitude and this automatically draws further opportunities to you.

What can you do to really make a difference? You are just one person amongst billions. You could give to charity, but to actually volunteer for a charity is better because there is a real involvement. But that still doesn't quite address the issue that, all around, others are behaving as they always have with little responsibility and you need to be a positive influence in your local community.

In so many avenues of modern life, the big issues loom large and everyone must speak out when they see laws and principles being undermined and subverted by those who wish to lead us along retrograde paths. We must never acquiesce to what is done by governments in our name unless we truly believe it is for the greater good.

Remember, 'good karma' can be drawn on from those simple lives of pure devotion that will help transform the ruthless tendencies from the brutish ones, which may be threatening to take over our lives again now. Spiritual growth is a slow process and circumstances never make it easy. Opportunities keep trying to lure us into a little devious dealing. Fear keeps rising up to subvert some good intention. This is the purpose of each incarnation, to transcend these things by walking more firmly on the earth with the heart awake and fully engaged.

# 10
# Intricate Planning

**The Incarnation Unfolds**

In order that you can follow the way a destiny plan is carried through, let us return to the three major lives under consideration, the Egyptian slave trader, the Roman Centurion and the Maharaja's son, where a lack of respect for women was endemic. As the one doing the planning, you must devise the new life in such a way that all their extreme tendencies can be resolved and it is vital to introduce a gentler dynamic into the psyche early on.

A female life needs to be included that will pacify many of the harsh elements that other lives will bring forward in their turn. After a childhood spent under an authoritarian father, this young woman entered a nunnery where she prayed incessantly for the forgiveness of her 'sins' which, in fact, were not hers, but stemmed from the Egyptian and the Roman lives, where a callous disregard for the feelings of the ordinary citizens was expected. (The Indian life came later.) She lived a very solitary and devout life, and the loving aspect of her nature shone through to her 'family' of nuns. There were no prickly relationships that so often breed in these cloistered places, at least not with her.

This ordered contemplative existence had gradually distanced her from the life outside the convent. She firmly believed that a strict path of abstinence would successfully deal with all the shameful things she sensed lay in the deep recesses of her soul and that God would truly forgive her. But, she didn't realize that approval could not be achieved by rejecting her 'sinful nature'; remember, that the dark and the light are one.

"I am here only for my Maker," she vowed, but her surroundings did not provide a wider reality to extend her achievements into. It needed a past life of lowered disposition to draw near in his astral body to put her developing love to the test.

The outworking of karma requires the one on Earth and the one in spirit to work harmoniously together, for they are both projections of the same source self. If the nun were to push away what she saw as her sinful nature, then this male past life would be forced to keep his distance and the second stage of the process, reconciliation with the outer world, could not be entirely achieved.

So, the centurion of old approached the nun's energy field, a small step at a time, which is the way it should be done, and entered respectfully into her times of personal devotion. By not fighting against her Christian attitudes too much, he used the heightened energy she had built up around her to release quite a lot of the aggressive tendencies he still harboured.

It was difficult for the nun to relate to this. She certainly felt an outpouring of compassion for her 'family' within the convent walls, but she was not completely able to forgive those men who fight wars and oppress others. Unconditional love still eluded her. There were limits to what she could do in the cloistered situation. The paucity of aggressive men in her life meant that her ability to be truly accepting of them remained largely untested. Simple devotion was not enough to complete the process.

The centurion needed to approach closer and then closer still, until she came to realise that she was capable of rejecting God, and could even kill innocent people. She did not understand why these feelings were there and these revelations were profoundly shocking for her.

She prayed and prayed for all Christians caught up in conflicts around the globe, yet her sense of culpability remained. She felt that she was taking on the mantle of the beloved Virgin bearing the sins of mankind. She did not give up her devotion, and gradually the inner pain was eased. A great deal of the barbaric nature of the centurion was also relieved. For the first time, she felt true forgiveness and, in turn, he discovered the quality of respect.

Now, it was the turn of the Egyptian to approach. Since his days on Earth, he had put a great deal of effort into his search for greater understanding, and in the period when slave trading was practised in Africa, he worked around a later incarnation of his, involved in this way of life, hoping to get him to exercise a more humane approach to the rights and welfare of the indigenous people under his control. However, the cruel and oppressive ways were, by this time, heavily ingrained and he was only partially successful.

The nun's growing acceptance of a brutal male presence in her aura was severely tested. She felt that there was something about this new energy that had depravity bleeding through every pore; it was deeply repugnant to her. There had been something cleaner and more straightforward about the Roman life.

Consequently, she was unable to extend her new-found ability to forgive to the clasp of corruption that accompanied this Egyptian life. She put up strong and determined defences against what she felt again to be an unacceptable side of herself, and prayed constantly for her own redemption. This did not include the salvation of this former life, so progress was largely denied him.

**Another opportunity**
It is interesting to note that, in the planned incarnation in Glasgow, one of the renunciates from that nunnery is to be the boy's teacher in the strict religious school that he will attend. And, from the inner levels, the nun will be able to encourage this woman to be a very supportive and understanding influence that could reform the lad's hostile attitude to religion and the generally accepted moral codes. (There are always moderating factors built into the destiny pattern, otherwise the life would become far too skewed towards the negative.)

So, another opportunity has been granted the slave-trader, and he needs to transmit a higher will into the young man growing up in that Glasgow vicarage for them both to effect a full release from the karma that he brings. It is not easy to relay new levels of understanding down, for much of the pain inflicted by him in his Egyptian incarnation will automatically rise up to invade their efforts, particularly when the lad accompanies his father on his pastoral duties into deprived areas where sympathy is required.

On the astral levels, the nun and the Egyptian had resolved

many of their differences, and both of them are hoping to bring a true Christian morality to the lad, while at the same time releasing a surge of reconciliation from the oversoul down through him into the earth. But you can be sure that the old antipathy of the nun towards the slave trader will be intensified as they get close—two strong, determined souls once again at loggerheads. Although they are trying in their own ways to instill compassionate attitudes into the young man's subconscious mind to facilitate release, initially it will be like a wedge has been slammed between them, preventing co-operation on the physical level until the goodwill of the present life releases them both.

The intense aversion to 'sin' established during the life in the nunnery, is felt to be 'religious hogwash' by the young man, and when his sister decides to spend her gap year in Africa helping to bring social justice to the people there, he is unsupportive. His indifference towards the troubles of people caught in poverty increases when he meets up with youngsters from poorer backgrounds who are from his extended spirit family, including some of the former slaves. The various relationships re-activate past frictions and escalate the inner battle being waged.

The young man, by now, is feeling something of an outsider and, when the nun's resolve wavers a little, he begins to develop an even more arrogant nature, turning increasingly away from the suffering of others. Deep down he knows that this is sliding him towards a repetition of past failings and, for a time, he tries to resist. However, the guilt and shame he feels, intensifies every time these callous attitudes are expressed, and he shuts down access to his heart to deal with it.

Pushing down the wayward impulses never works for long, and obsessive behaviour inevitably took over. The way out was to balance his heart before stepping forward judiciously, letting the temptations fall behind. In this case, the old attitudes were strongly there by the time he embarked on a business studies course at a London university.

"I intend doing exactly as I wish. As a budding entrepreneur I will do anything it takes to give me an advantage," is set against the nun's, "I must follow the dictates of my conscience and resist those who would tempt me into immoral behaviour." These two intentions are irreconcilable. This is why the conscience in some people is so profoundly distressing; there are two separate past lives at war within them.

By the time he gets to Florida, it is not yet a lost cause, but his brother wants him to get involved in a business that is promoting genetically modified crops. This gives him many taxing moral issues to address and his dilemma is exacerbated by his former life as a botanist who is still very concerned about these matters.

The challenges have come before an enhanced moral stance is securely in place, much too early for him, in fact, and when the influence of the Egyptian life increases, the seductive appeal of his former scurrilous nature causes him to slip and slide before he eventually succumbs to it.

The nun is struggling to convert her antipathy towards the Egyptian slaver into love for all those he has harmed, knowing that, without this, the progress of her oversoul and all the lives supported by it, will be held back.

**A way out**
You have surely heard of those religious people who, even today, carry out self flagellation. What an extreme approach this is, for the great master's request to love all sinners must start with loving what you despise in yourself. Only then can this love be reflected out to include all the people you've harmed who are now closely involved with you.

To pray and meditate regularly is not always practical in this hectic modern world. In the old days, of course, people engaged in normal life for six days a week and the seventh was kept for worship and quiet reflection. This provided some respite from the pressures of a world that had scant respect for the spiritual. Otherwise, it required super-human effort to resist the multitude of temptations crowding in.

To try to be a saint before you can actually live it, only leads to despair at the failure. It is essential to release the virulent energies

*Intricate Planning*

that rise up whenever perfection is sought, to dance, sing, and celebrate without recourse to drugs and alcohol; to let the wind sweep through your hair as you sit on a cliff top watching the sunset. It is by getting back to simple pleasures that the heaviness of the past is most effectively released. Children do it spontaneously, but adults often forget how to be young at heart, to laugh at themselves when life gets too serious, to rejoice and release all cares to an understanding and forgiving universe. It's only a start, but an effective one.

Also, remember that it is what you give to others, unselfishly and without conditions, that most effectively frees you from your pain. Service does not have to be experienced as drudgery. It can be a joy when undertaken in the right frame of mind. Then you can bring upliftment to those who have sunk low, and you bring down to earth those who have gone too high, which may well include one of your own former lives.

If you are truly in your heart, don't be apprehensive about letting a past life consciousness enter your aura. It may take you over a bit and trigger off adverse reactions from those around you. Anger erupts, you are shouted at and abused, tears may flow, but if you respond quietly, and don't race in to comfort or explain, something will mature in you both. By being present for others, simply, without manipulation, a new strength of purpose eases out some of the old long-standing karma.

Releasing pent-up energies is so important; this great universe is quite large enough to cope when you hand your shadow energies over to the elements. It is when vitriol and judgement are inflicted on people that the karmic repetitions occur.

If you do anything that you inwardly perceive as 'wrong' and guilt rises up, and you feel trapped between two strong impulses, do not close down or defend yourself against either. And, certainly do not speed up, hoping to avoid it that way, because soon your life will be going nowhere fast. The solution is to love both aspects of yourself equally, the wilfully expressive part and the part that avoids true involvement. Unconditional love, waiting to express itself through you, seeks balance above all else. It is clearly stated in the bible "Love thy neighbour as thyself," although that isn't as easy as it sounds.

Some people become missionaries, going door to door in an attempt to convert people to their belief system; they feel that then it will be easier to love them. Or they might keep away from anything they feel would challenge their ideas and upset their defences, which the truth always does. Any extreme energies coming in from the past will lead a person into excess of some kind, and the life in Florida was to have many periods of indulgence.

If the 'nun' incarnation in you has been pushed to the background and is having a difficult time making her presence felt, more quiet time on your own is called for. Her humility is worth opening up to. Avoid falling into the trap of belittling those around you in an attempt to make yourself appear more worthy.

Negotiating a safe path in this somewhat unstable world requires an active neutrality. Gandhi did not hate the English when he faced up to them, he understood them very well and above all, he did respect them. When you take sides and condemn, you actually give power to what you oppose. Strident pacifists are often closet warmongers. Whatever you hate in the world is certainly there within you.

**The Shadow Band**
The state of 'no judgement' is difficult to achieve. At this time, vast numbers of people have invited some 'least aware' past lives to come close, hoping to free themselves from their most damaging excesses at last. As the Aquarian energies become stronger over the years immediately ahead, the shadow will increase its determination to infiltrate our defences and block every ray of light we are trying to focus into our lives.

Increase the light and the forces of disruption are certain to be aroused inside you and around you. That is the crux. When the divine light begins to reveal what lies hidden, the shadow is certain to be there whispering seductively, cajoling you, trying to infiltrate your mind with its usual plethora of lies. The shadow is a malignant force within the cosmos, an artful schemer that insidiously attaches itself to the entirely natural dark component of our human nature, perverting it to its own ends. It is proving a more than worthy adversary for, today, a considerable number of souls are still being drawn into its web of deceit.

You have heard the expression 'let sleeping dogs lie.' You try to keep everything in check by dealing with the issues methodically but, with each successive wave increasing the intensity, you may feel you cannot cope. But keep going, for unless it is genuinely too heavy a load, it is wise not to 'let sleeping dogs lie' for they only gain the confidence to bite you harder, later on.

The shadow band of spirits does not have any moral scruples; they enjoy tricking people into putting shades up against the light that will filter and lessen its influence and benefit. So, you need to keep your wits about you and encourage your better nature to grow and assert itself. And, even then, it won't be all plain sailing for, as humanity progresses, the intrusions of the shadow band become more subtle. They are directing their efforts towards every vulnerable human heart, but especially towards those people committed to service who still harbour a secret craving for power.

Whenever the light is deflected, the shadow will come forward to impersonate the light. The anti-Christ, when he comes, will no longer preach war, but peace and love—peace, that is, at a price. He isn't a fool; he knows what people want to hear, but it will be a cold, egoistic kind of love.

Uncovering the deceptive ways of the shadow is a big challenge for those seeking the light today. There are many warmongers who proclaim peace as their goal. Humankind has heard all this before and will again, so long as the tit-for-tat attitudes remain. If you can frustrate your 'enemy' to act precipitously, then you can justify retaliatory action but, of course, this is the great hypocrisy, perpetrated even at the highest levels of planetary governance today and its message is very attractive to the unenlightened masses.

### Finding Balance

An excessively stern father can create problems for a child, but so can an over-indulgent mother. Love comprises two components, the firm and the compassionate, and it is necessary to ensoul both. You say to your child, "Don't do that, dear" and when this is understood and accepted, the arms go round and assurance is given. Too many people today, believe that 'love' is just the warm embracing part. They need to learn the art of caring detachment. Kids don't want their parents to be part of their world, they just want a strong, loving parental influence to be there when they need it.

Marriage can provide a potent opportunity to learn how to effect union within yourself so that, in all lives that follow, the polarised extremes will no longer hold sway and the energies will oscillate close to the middle way, even when the situation around is in turmoil.

Socialism is seen as the enemy of capitalism, but it is a false perspective. The true way is not one thing or its converse, it is always the best of both, alternating in influence. It is about learning to blend the two together, the yin and the yang, the power from above and the power from below, you and everything else, into an effective working relationship.

It is time to take on the qualities of non-judgement, gratitude, and respect. To move onto a higher level it is also necessary to cultivate a greater simplicity within that can find its place in the greater complexity building up outside. It is about forging a personal path that, at times, will appear to be incompatible with the soul's basic objectives. Nothing can be completed until the incarnation has reached a point when the synthesis of both sides of a particular experience or way of life can be achieved, and when the outer reality welcomes this.

Now, the nun and the abusive slave trader—who, remember, are two aspects from the same source consciousness—did not manage a complete reconciliation when close to the physical environment. Their coming together achieved on the astral level was not extended into the current reality, and the time has come for the nun to retreat from close proximity to the Earth. In the next phase, the woman who was the slave trader's wife in that Egyptian time is to be the past life influence behind his wife again, in this.

## The Crunch Comes

In Florida, some material success was achieved under his brother's wing and while some of the opportunities available to him could have been realised by gradual means, others required moral corners to be cut. Alas, the ruthless elements from the Egyptian past took over once again.

Our man was in his element. To him, money is all and the people who do not believe that are fools. Well, needless to say, he met up with the businessman, who would have been his father from the outset, if the other choice of parents had been made. However, though married, it is this man's daughter that attracted him most, for she was the female servant he favoured in Egypt.

When the life was being planned, it had been hoped that by now he would have overcome many of the harsh attitudes that the Egyptian life was bringing to him, and he would be well equipped to deal with the even more extreme energies of the Indian life that were beginning to come forward. But the necessary moral development hadn't happened and a growing belligerence carried our man into a particularly ruthless, acquisitive stage that fitted nicely into the rampant American economy of that time.

This life has yet to run its course. Various strands of his past have converged along with the great economic shifts in the world economy, and there is a major make-or-break crisis looming for him shortly—one which was inevitable, when you consider the karma undermining it.

During this transition time from one age to another, a much greater spiritual light is shining in, and all of the selfish impulses in human nature are being aroused into even more extreme positions in their ultimately futile attempts to block it. From the inner and outer turmoil that is engulfing us, a massive global awakening is possible and much more effective ways of proceeding. Is this happening? Are the torch bearers in the upper echelons of power standing up, Gandhi-like, to the multi-national cartels? Alas, not yet. It is being left to the grass-roots initiatives to make the changes.

When the dark element grounds higher energies in physical reality, these extremely acquisitive systems must collapse, because their power was built up through imbalance. When the light workers on this planet really find their strength, the power of the shadow ones to reap havoc will run out. But they are not giving up easily and the inevitable confrontations are leaving many casualties. Our man in Florida is heading for a very rude awakening.

It is interesting to note that the brother's new partner had been the young cousin installed as Maharaja in India instead of him. You can't get away from the past, it surrounds you, it has led you to where you are, and wishes to remain the dominant influence. However, when you have aroused the will to act in accordance with your heart's dictates, this will highlight some aspect of your nature needing to be understood and expressed in a completely new way.

**The Early Influences**
Individuality goes far beyond the personality. Individuality is of the spirit, personality lies with the soul, and these two have got to combine to carry forward the plan. The personality develops first in the baby; individuality usually comes to the fore around the age of seven. Alas, from the very beginning, many parents project their hopes and frustrations into their child, instilling ideas of success and failure, those two great deceivers that always obscure the wise part of us. And, so the personality grows into a false one. It would be wrecking the plan to be able to look backwards and forwards beyond our ability to assimilate what is revealed to us, and we are constantly being encouraged to do this by those who wish to complicate our human experience in order to gain more power for themselves.

And, what about these former lives operating from the spirit realms, who often feel considerable frustration when things don't proceed as they hoped? Are they going to encourage the child to be less ambitious? Unlikely. This often leads to a sense of failure persistently undermining all present endeavours. So, you can see how much we inherit from our past, with inappropriate encouragement from both worlds carrying it forward. (In your adult life, it is useful to contact your inner child to tell it that it doesn't have to be successful.)

Karmic energy is incomplete energy, and there is ultimately no point in trying to prevent it coming through from a former part of you. It is needed; let it in and convert it into the constructive energy required for you both to move forward. You are in it together. If you are experiencing pain, the one on the spirit side who instigated the karma is certainly suffering far more.

Goodwill towards your own inner self must be expanded generously to include all other soul parts of the greater you. To see deeply into your past will awaken an element within that registers future possibilities that lie beyond the limits of destiny. We can access these transforming streams of energy and allow them to take charge. It has nothing to do with desire or wishful thinking, nothing to do with persuading yourself that you were once very important and must be again. Disaster lies on that path because you are living in a fantasy world that you have built up around yourself—not the reality that the Divine Creator has offered you to carry your evolution forward.

**Changes to the Plan**
When you operate on the astral level in your sleeping hours, that part of you regularly reviews your progress on Earth. From there, you can mentally link up with any of your past lives to adjust and redirect a particular life stream for your mutual benefit.

You can imagine what goes on in these nightly sojourns, the confrontations that sometimes take place. For instance, you don't think a former life of yours is doing enough to ease your pain, and you tell him so in no uncertain terms. He will probably retaliate and suggest that you are not spending enough time on the issues that concern him, you are avoiding his karma, and this, he says, has stranded him between worlds. He is really very annoyed. (When past personalities resonate with the Earth's atmosphere, they become almost human again.)

You are discovering that some forces are stronger than expected. Even though the plan was set in place by a soul personality who had quite recently left the Earth, the wilful nature of the emotional temperaments may already have been forgotten.

Before you incarnated, it was expected that you would easily resolve a tricky situation that would arise due to the thoughtless actions of one of your past lives many centuries ago. You came with high hopes and full spirit backing, but now that you are actually in that situation, your determination has deserted you. This often happens. You move enthusiastically towards some group or situation where there is karma, only to drift away soon after. An escapist element convinces you that it wasn't the right place for you, when, in fact, it was important to continue.

Usually, it is a combination of over-optimism on the part of the past personalities planning your life, and the lack of discipline on your part in preparing for the challenges to come. Sometimes, there may not be much you can do about it in the short term. Your early resolve will remain in tatters until the necessary adjustments have been made to get your past life more finely attuned to you. Until then, there will be an inevitable delay in the resolution. There is no point in regretting your past stumbles. The energetic mix is very hard to get right. Don't blame yourself if there was a miscalculation or if the laziness bug got to you for a time, it happens.

Karmic issues do not automatically flow from one life into the next. Unresolved fragments of your past are drawn from different incarnations, often hundreds of years apart, and there may be some connection missing. The energies aren't always flowing smoothly between them, and you feel fragmented and indecisive. There are so many reasons why it takes longer than you would wish, and to get impatient with your progress is a total waste of energy.

The way to deal with a karmic situation is to not see it as a battle. You must disassociate yourself from what happened before, otherwise it will assume you're giving it the right to resume the offensive. You are entirely responsible for removing all negative participation from your side of it, but no more. As you link into the earth, and detach, the remaining energy of it will be released back to the vast universe where it will be received gratefully; your new-found freedom celebrated and the 'sin' forgiven.

Sometimes, when a particular piece of karma has been dealt with successfully, the past life involved may try to get you to move onto

## Intricate Planning

another area of that same incarnation which had not originally been agreed to, and because there had been so much involvement in that past energy, it had almost become part of you and so, it may be difficult to detach from it entirely.

Certain people, in a variety of guises, crop up again and again. Some are allies but others bring a destructive energy that has been magnified and extended in many lives, relived rather than relieved. And now one of them has arrived in your life, bringing several past lives in tow and a whole raft of issues involving honesty, jealousy, domination—and your own past lives are there, overshadowing you, champing at the bit.

Encourage only one at a time to come close. If they both bear in on you, it will generate more stress than you can handle, and if the other person involved is also over-zealous, you may have to take determined measures to deal with the pressure. In such cases, ask the past lives to behave with more consideration, project such thoughts to them. In that inner sense, you need to take firm control of your life.

Mentally assert your needs, and before going to sleep, determine that there will be a meeting with the minds of all the spirit world participants. Instruct your inner mind to get one of them, at least, to back off. But what if they are all fired up by this opportunity to 'deal with' an old adversary and they refuse? For your life to run smoothly, those past lives must respect your situation and take your actual ability to cope into account. If they won't, there is little you can do to lessen the load except to keep sending out further thoughts to them, not as a victim, but as the one who has been granted free will on this level with the right to determine what your life should be.

The converse of this—un-ambitious past lives—is just as problematic. You are motivated, you wish to forge a progressive life but the inner support you require is not there. You experience low level distress on a constant basis, nothing seems to be entirely clear or moving well. But, sometimes it is the other people in your life and their former lives who are letting you down.

Before your life, the Lords of Karma gave their blessing to a particular relationship. The two of you made contact in your sleep state and agreed to activate a meeting in the human course of events. You are ready, your past lives are ready, but when you do meet, the other person says, "No, thank you" and backs away. There is no choice but to swallow your pride and put off this karmic outworking to a later time.

**The World Is Changing**
In the old days, people stayed married for an entire life and this was planned for. Both participants would undertake a gradual preparation for a union twenty or more years ahead, and the slow pace of those times meant that it usually came about as planned and developed subsequently along intended lines. Nevertheless, many people stayed together long after love had died, because of the children or because it was expected of them. It is no longer, 'till death do us part' but 'until the reason for our coming together has been fulfiled'.

It is useless for people to bemoan the down-grading of marriage. This is a time when souls are attempting to bring the various strands of past experience into an integrated whole, and it is unlikely that one person can provide all that is needed. You live in a global world, which tells you that your Chinese life and your Russian life and your South American life, and so on, are coming together in a kind of 'United Nations' within you.

Here is another actual example to consider. A man is wondering why all his relationships have ended abruptly and, in some cases, acrimoniously. He had been linked up with a very attractive woman for awhile. She had been an unfaithful wife in seventeenth century Russia. They travelled to Moscow on business and both felt at home there, but a charming, persuasive and rich man came into her life, a minor oligarch caught up in the financially liberated atmosphere following the fall of the Berlin Wall. He had the cunning to exploit it and she respected that.

There was an instant soul recognition. She thought it was love she was feeling, but it was mere infatuation, a welcome contrast to her own rather mundane existence. "He is the man of my dreams," she believed, but this relationship was not meant to replace the existing one. He was a ship passing in the night. Certainly she was dazzled and swept away by him, but he was all surface commitment. He was someone she had adored, at a distance, in another life when he was a Lord and she, a humble servant. "One day, he will be mine," she thought, and now the opportunity has presented itself. She does not realise that he will use her and then drop her, for he is that kind of person.

"Don't leave your husband. Can't you see what he is like?" is called down from the spirit world by the support team. But she leaves her husband anyway and, of course, it doesn't work out. A time of reappraisal is needed.

Some people look for what they had in the past, trying to re-establish the situations where it seemed to work, not realising that a quite different way forward is required now. In such circumstances, the soul is prevented from sending out a clear statement of need to the world and, in this case, a replacement was not there because she had to come into some understanding of what had happened before another opportunity could arise. Otherwise, it would be a repetition of the past circumstances and the same end result.

A life needs to be a progression in all possible ways, and the abandoned husband was afforded exactly the kind of replacement he needed to take him forward. That is the rule. Where a person is ready, life is compelled to respond.

His next relationship was with a woman who had aborted him in eighteenth century Peru. She was overly maternal towards him and this was, of course, based in guilt. She treated him like a dependent child, smothering him with her protective love. His lesson was to discover his sense of self worth, assert himself and then break away, which he eventually did.

Each fragment from the past only required a few years of close proximity to resolve the negative residues of karma, at least, his side of it. In those two lives, the karmic imbalance was in his favour, but then he attracted a wife from a recent Spanish incarnation. He had not respected her as a person of equal worth, and her latent talent for fine needlework was totally suppressed.

What happened then? A great deal of progress was made, in fact. He confronted his old chauvinistic patterns and she made sure that he responded unselfishly to her needs. If you met him today, you would see a much reformed character, not cynical at all. They married and went into business together in the rag trade. The karma to be faced now was entirely external to the relationship, stemming from a Scandinavian life where they had together done much damage to the stability of their local community.

As long as both the partners continue to bring a generosity of spirit to the relationship, everything will be fine. In very few partnerships is the karma entirely one sided and, even if it is, karma cannot be completed without a full reconciliation by the two parties. No matter how horrendous the act that was perpetrated, mutual love and respect is still required from both the damaged one and the perpetrator.

(It is interesting to note, when considering the karma incurred during the Second World War, that it is not so much the Germans from that time who are delaying the outworking in the spirit realms, it is many of the former Jews, who cannot forgive.)

**Adjustments to the Plan**
It is karmic bits and pieces now, the lifetime relationships of the past are not so often required, which means that everything is much more immediate and flexible. Many relationships founder because the two parties are drawn apart by quite different priorities, and there is no alternative but to move on.

Backup positions are usually allowed for in the destiny format if a break-up occurs. The blueprint for your life is a mixture of a few set elements, with specific people marked into the pattern to work on them, and many that are merely the kind of situation you need to face, that several, or many different people could participate in.

Whatever happens, new relationships have to take up roughly where the last one left off for both participants, and your search for the perfect partner may be a fruitless one. All of the initial prospects may have moved forward further or slower than you or into quite different avenues of interest.

So, what do you do if your intended partner or colleague defects? There are many possible close links featured in your destiny pattern which could be engaged in some kind of relationship. There were the former husbands and wives and lovers, and also those mothers, sisters, and friends for whom you had a special affection or antipathy, but their needs must fit exactly into the kind of life you are leading now; therefore, there is no certainty that any of them will still be willing to participate at all. If the divide is too great, there may be no value at all in a meeting. It would result in stagnation for one and too much pressure piled onto the other. Whether or not there is personal karma between you, their developmental priorities and capabilities must complement your own. Obscure alternatives may have to be considered, the net cast wider.

Opportunities may now appear in unfamiliar contexts, and you will have to keep a sharp eye out for them. Those working under the Lords of Karma are constantly watching over events and seeking out people who might play a useful role in your life, though some of their past lives might need a lot of convincing. "Do I really want to become involved with that loser?" may be the initial, very human-like, response.

You can't always keep the flow going. Unexpected factors come in that leave you floundering or stranded in some respect and, on this slow physical plane, it can take some time for a replacement to be found and manoeuvred into place.

Ultimately, the exact person is less important than what is brought to the relationship, and sometimes quite unlikely people are able to provide the necessary ingredients. Possibly, when one opportunity is passed up or passes on by, it may be found that there is no replacement available who precisely fits the bill. It may have to be shared among a number of people, each taking on one facet of the issue to be faced.

## The Patterns Are Flexible

The destiny plan is a blueprint for the life ahead, a basic framework, with much of the detail dependent on the actions of people exercising their free will; it allows for this. There are many variables in a life pattern, others cannot be altered. The natural size and the shape of the physical body is genetically proscribed, but what happens to it, by way of serious illnesses, for example, can sometimes delay or modify the destined outworking and even affect the spiritual possibilities in ways that were not anticipated. Many details of the life, even crucial ones, must be left to the vagaries of fate.

In these turbulent, fast-moving times, it is impossible to know, for certain, what is going to happen next year. There are so many ways things might go in unexpected directions. For example, the economy collapses and the job you thought was secure is lost. Was that predicted before you were born? Probably not, for though the direction of the main forces operating in you and in the situations around you would have been clear back then, the precise detail needed to wait.

Deviations from the plan can magnify to such an extent that the outworking of the destiny envisioned has to be totally rethought, with different people, a different country even, being called for. There are many people living unmarried lives, when it is in their destiny to have tied the knot long ago. But circumstances changed and they had to accept what is possible.

It is necessary to welcome the people and situations that come forward; accepting that they are the best available from the pool of possibility. You must remain optimistic, knowing that everything is being done by your team in spirit to orchestrate the most appropriate and propitious flow of events for your life at all times, even if it is not what you are expecting or, indeed, would wish for. It is important to remember that.

Take an actual life as an example. There was a man I knew, an American, who had engaged in brutal wars in a number of former lives and many people had suffered at his hands. In this life, his destiny indicated that he may have to endure some deformity, so that he would experience what it is like to be on the receiving end. However, there had been good acts done in some other lives that mitigated in his favour and so, it was not a foregone conclusion. During the birth, the mother was prescribed a drug that would have caused physical abnormalities, but the affirmative energies came in alerting her to the dangers and the birth was a normal one. Later on, poliomyelitis came into his path. But once again, as he had demonstrated no hostility to his school mates—he did not fight, disrupt or rebel—this illness passed him by.

Then the Vietnam War came along. There was considerable conflict in the soul of this man. One side of him was against all kinds of killing, but the other felt that, perhaps, this war was a just one, and that his country needed him. He didn't think deeply about it. There was conscription, and he was one of those expected to comply. A tremendous pressure was put on him by his government and by public opinion. It was his duty, they said, to protect his country against the communist threat. Of course, he could have stood up to them, refused to 'serve', and taken the consequences, but he did not do this. He obeyed the command and, in that war, lost a leg.

You see, opportunities were there to resolve the karma without suffering, which were ultimately not taken up, but it can be reported that, through his infirmity, he did come to understand his karma and it was, in due course, fully resolved. It is always good to report a happy ending.

# 11
# Resolving the Issues

**Working Together**
Advanced occult knowledge was once entirely esoteric, practised by alchemists in their laboratories, high priests in their temples, and witches in their covens. Today, these things are more out in the open and easily distorted by those seeking unwarranted recognition, while making a lot of money for themselves in the process. They add impressive, but unnecessary, detail and complexity to the teachings not realising that ideas of profound simplicity can best illuminate the path of those who are lost and need guidance.

I have stressed that the solution to many of life's challenges requires a collaboration with one of your former lives linking up with you from the inner planes. Without that, there can be no complete resolution. Then there are those people you meet along the way where a friendship develops that is karmically based. Your friend will have a past consciousness positioned in the background as well, and the two former lives who created the karma need to resolve their differences as the relationship develops. However, when these two approach the Earth atmosphere, they are forced apart and cannot easily deal with the old hostility rising up or drawn too close, too tight, where there was dependency before.

If you don't treat this as a spiritual opportunity more than an earthly one, then you can easily get caught up in past struggles and the awkward nature of the physical relationship, the lack of rapport, the fiery energies that are aroused could result in more negative karma being added to the lot already incurred.

It is important to be detached, not caught up too much in the need to sort things out. It may be a serious situation but it requires a deftness of touch. Encourage your friend to detach also, so that the two past lives can re-engage in the present without either of you getting too involved.

Karma incurred on Earth must be released on Earth, and as these earlier souls cannot incarnate again, it is you, the current representative, who is acting as a conduit for the outworking. You want a resolution, but even though you may sense the issues that were active when this blockage was incurred, don't get caught up in the detail; it is just energy of a particular kind working its way out through you now.

Remember, you didn't do it. You're helping someone else out. You're the channel for the energies to come through, that's all. It is so important to separate the responsibility because you needn't carry a burden of guilt and shame that you wrongly believe is yours.

There'll be a great deal of inner disturbance while the energy adjustments are being carried out, which can take weeks, or months, but if you don't get involved in what is happening on that inner level and if you remain unconcerned about the outcome, then you will more easily recognize the lesson to be learnt from it and the resolution will be as swift and peaceful as it can be.

**Wasted Lives**

Of course, you have had wasted lives when you ignored the promptings from spirit and did not follow a useful path. You exercised you free will and just idled your life away.

In perhaps two or three percent of cases, individual souls or even an entire group of souls may choose to go against the laws of karma entirely, often at the last minute. They are advised to wait a little, but a surge of ego demands, "No, it needs to happen now", and the birth happens at an inappropriate time for the incarnation to unfold as it should.

The place is the right one and there are matters to work out, but on arrival, these souls can't relate to their surroundings, they don't fit in because the other participants aren't incarnate yet or aren't ready. So, these premature people wander around, living very mechanical lives, feeling out of place, out of time; they just can't seem to get anything to work out for them. However, if they follow a path of service and develop attributes that will be needed later, they will eventually find the opportunity to participate. Until then, they cannot force themselves into a life that is not welcoming them.

There is a more extreme, but rare scenario where a soul group is so determined to have another incarnation that they reject the participation of the Lords of Karma entirely. They are extremely irrational and forceful in their demands. They intend to incarnate directly from the lower levels of the astral plane before the full assimilation of the previous life has been completed and the cause of their self-destructive behaviour identified. They want more Earth experience and are unwilling to wait.

The urge to return becomes like an addiction and they manage to manipulate their way into a new body that is quite unprepared for the kinds of difficulties it will have to experience. They may push a gentle soul that is preparing for a life in a particular body right out of the way, taking over the moment of conception instead. Needless to say, there are disastrous consequences.

I know of one case where a soul commandeered a female body that wasn't hers to have and it consistently failed to function properly. In her fourteenth year she had her ovaries removed, in her twenty fifth, she began to have epileptic fits, and it became more serious until she eventually passed from a stroke. There is certainly a wiser soul there now as it approaches the life that should have been, that now has so much extra to deal with because of that impulsiveness. Indeed, the whole life will be devoted to accepting and working with the body being occupied.

**Incarnations Not Necessarily Wasted**
I need to distinguish here between those lives where people, for some reason, did not attain what they set out to accomplish, and those that needed very minimal human interaction, in an isolated farming community perhaps. These simple lives are not necessarily wasted ones. It is possible to live a quiet, uncomplicated existence and cultivate a deep inner connection with Mother Earth as a source of spiritual strength. Other lives of this kind may be chosen to consolidate a past achievement in a confined environment,

a single man cooped up a university laboratory, perhaps, before engaging with more far-reaching applications in a later life.

Whenever you are contained in a very restricted compass of experience, the inner worlds are very active. A renunciate nun would be communing exclusively with the spirit within, where the devotional aspect had been neglected in a former life of this kind.

Everyone has a completely unique reason for choosing a particular way of progression. Sometimes it is appropriate to continue with that journey right through to life's end, and sometimes it is necessary to move beyond it.

There are lives, however, when the person has no choice—those shut away in mental homes, those who are blind, who are deaf, who are in physical bodies that are not perfect. There is a common belief that these handicaps are all karmic conditions brought about by some unwise behaviour in the past, but this is not necessarily so. Some old souls have voluntarily incarnated into a restricted condition to give certain people the opportunity to learn a valuable lesson.

Whenever a great work of service is undertaken in this way, it follows that there are many on Earth linked up to those in spirit working on that particular plan. Some very advanced souls who need an Earth anchor, will incarnate with a body and a brain that is not complete so that the greater part of themselves may operate fully on higher levels. A normally expressive life would prevent this inner purpose being carried out, so the mind and body on Earth must be subdued. Though the great majority of Downes' Syndrome children are young souls, a few are very advanced and engaged in high service to the planet, usually alongside some more personal karma being worked out. Often, there is the need for the parents to learn to love that one unconditionally.

Other old souls use telepathy from the higher planes to inspire human channels in many branches of the teaching, healing, and creative arts. This is the Law of Progression—for the chain of service extends right down even into the darkest places, which can only be reached by specially trained people operating in physical bodies.

The very highest expression of the Christ presence, so far, in human form, came to show us how we might support our weaker brethren. This does not mean that we necessarily need to carry younger souls on our shoulders. It is more often done by standing back and directing power to them at a frequency just beyond their ability to consciously receive, and this will help them register a more responsible way of proceeding. Everything is passed down from on high to those in need in the most effective ways possible.

To be in a reasonably healthy physical body with normal levels of ambition means taking on material responsibilities and treading a pathway that is definitely outgoing. As you advance, you attain a fine balance between the material and the spiritual. Young souls, the majority of people on the planet today, have to find the spiritual entirely through trial and error, the more advanced ones can evolve through joyous interaction.

At this point, I suggest that you contemplate your true nature. You are clearly more than just bits and pieces of your past lives flung together in a new combination or a creative spark that is forever lighting flames of ever increasing luminosity. It is not just that you are linked up to an essence that supports you, you *are* that essence. Even though the source self is consistently blending all the various identities into one unified nature, individuality is never destroyed. We are all unique examples of the one being two and the two being one, the universal matrix manifesting separately but not actually separate. In other words, the sole divinity of which you are a part, has allowed you to be a sole divinity in your own right.

**Past-life Therapy**
If you are struggling to surrender to the here and now, if a certain reluctance is preventing higher steams of consciousness reaching you from your spirit self, if you are out of balance and an attachment to worldly concerns is preventing a full reconciliation between you and the relevant past personalities, then some form of past-life therapy may be called for. Let us look at three ways this can be entered into.

*Resolving the Issues*

If you regularly reach up in meditation in your search for greater understanding and you wish to contact the masters of the rays who can help you release the past, then regression through hypnotherapy might suit you. So relax, slow down, attune and allow. Slow down? Yes, this is important. When your mind speeds up, you move away from your essence towards unfamiliar realms and realities that are not yet ready to be there for you.

A fine balance is achieved when the human rhythm slowly alternates and the faster world of spirit impinges on your human sensibility. If you send your mind off into the non-physical realms without grounding yourself, the fear of losing control can unsettle you. If you slow down instead and separate off the two streams of consciousness—the human part of you reaching down with the spiritual part reaching up—then, with each new breath, a greater unity becomes possible. A depth of awareness, a precise inner perception of how things really are, can then be extracted from between this apparent separation and channelled through into all areas of your life and to all the previous lives involved.

Of course, the therapist will be well skilled in protection, but the most secure boundaries can only be provided by the individuals themselves. To be reliable, 'past-life' therapists need to have both the yin and the yang parts of themselves quite well balanced, as both aspects are required in the process. They need to have worked through a great deal of the impulsiveness that was once aroused when their own dark side was over-assertive for they will need to hold a very secure line for a client who is wavering. You can trust them because they have been to the edge themselves and know what can occur there.

You will be asked to breathe slowly and align yourself to your heart. Your human involvement is then subdued, enabling you to focus deep within and, from there, to reach in and link with another consciousness reaching out to you. The degree of non-involvement determines the purity of the communication. The Earth consciousness is still present, though stilled; awareness remains and, in this state of reverie, your focussed mind can approach towards where a particular former life is positioned.

Some therapists take you on a journey and ask questions. "What are you seeing? Which country are you in? What does your body feel like? Describe it," and so on. That way, a picture is built up of the surrounding reality and you can enter into a deep attunement with something of what that person was. But, because the Earth mind has to follow these instructions, it will be involved in the outcome, and this means that the inner contact is unlikely to be a pure one. Flashes of past life memory come in, and these are built on by the imagination.

It is important to understand that, during hypnosis, your astral mind can direct thought lines into your brain that can 'speak' to you and through you. It is not a direct past life communication; your astral self is absorbing the energies and converting them into ideas that you can use. This has value, for then the energy behind any misguided beliefs, any unsound attitudes, or the constrictions that were there, can be released through you.

You could be taken from conception right through to the moment of death, picking out important events along the way. To be useful, these need to relate to the present life. They can explain a phobia, an arthritic knee, an aversion, or a difficult relationship. Then the journey under hypnosis opens out to include family, friends, and those who bear you a grudge. "Is there anyone involved that you know today? What does this tell you?" and so on. The therapist probably has a prepared list of questions that will lead you into the kind of detail that you can respond to.

Then you will be brought gently back and encouraged to retain this understanding so that the integration process can continue on both the physical and soul levels once you have returned to 'normal life'. Such a procedure depends not only on the willingness of the client to surrender, but also on the unflinching discipline of the therapist. It can be a great help on issues that are not too steeped in the harshness of the shadow, and particularly useful where the former life was female.

The most effective therapists are primarily of a yang nature, with a good measure of yin to back it up, and the model client is essentially yin with a good measure of yang. An insufficiently grounded yin therapist may inadvertently encourage a client who is prone to fantasy, to let this element take over.

I strongly recommend that two therapists work in tandem, one the sensitive, the other the protector and healer. It is difficult for one person to juggle both aspects, particularly where the karma involves violence rather than vanity. If the dark, lowering forces are intruding too strongly, invoking bleak, frightening images, the therapist must be grounded and able to 'hold' the client securely as the wild energies are released.

The attunement between the past and present life can easily be shattered by fear rising up; and any sudden jolt to either would make it difficult to continue. In such cases, hypnotherapy may not be the best way to proceed. Where there are heavy masculine energies or obsessions involved, the past personality may need to come in closer to achieve a full release and this would require very strong therapists able to bring the client into a precise alignment down which the former self can descend.

**A Past Life Speaks**

With a particularly sensitive client, who is somewhat psychic and not too fearful of the dark, it may be possible for the therapist to enable the past personality to enter into the client's aura where it will be able to speak more directly. The less involved the client is, the more effective the communication, so the therapist will tell the client not to pay any attention to what is being said. This requires a tremendous amount of stillness and balance in both participants, for such clients are channelling another part of themselves and the therapist must respond on that level. Then it is almost as if one spirit consciousness is speaking to another.

When a past-life practitioner has a highly developed capacity for detachment, the client is drawn into a similar state. The past person has to feel free to say whatever it likes. What comes through is not always rational—it may come from a very amoral place where primitive energies and old thought processes still hold sway.

The discarnate one will be led gently to the point where the karmic energies are re-engaged and brought through into a confrontation with the yang psychic who is fully conscious of what needs to be done, so that the hidden issues can be revealed and resolved.

Imagine that someone who incited many people to fight a hated enemy is coming through. The client has always tried to live a peaceful and trustworthy life, but there was a soul heaviness that could not be lifted. Violent nightmares were frequently experienced. To let this warrior soul through, without balking, will require a great deal of courage. The therapist has to sensitively lead the past life to re-experience what happened, the actuality of it, and then, in the light of truth, much of the conflicted energy can be released.

Then, the therapist raises a hand, which may be holding a cross or ankh or some other powerful symbol, and asks the former life to look at the picture that is forming there. It could be the face of one of those who were harmed and guilt has kept the two of them apart. The perpetrator will be told that forgiveness has already been granted, although this may not be believed. The victim is then encouraged to manifest more clearly, smiling, with arms outstretched, and the two can make contact energetically in the pure light of love. This will lift a burden from both of them.

The client's former life is then shown the available opportunities for a fresh start. "What have you always wanted to do with your life? Would you like to go with your guardians to where you can be given the chance to develop this?" And then, taking advantage of the opening being provided by the therapist, the past entity is lifted up and taken to higher levels of experience.

This method is often by far the most efficient way of grounding and dispersing the energies of these very heavy Earth karmas, but the past entity needs to be completely ready to go through this process, or the bewildered client would not be able to cope with the intensity of it. Sometimes a minor life comes through first, so that confidence is built up to tackle the more difficult one later.

When the spirit entity is a much more uncooperative character and likely to cause trouble, a third approach can be used. Here, the client is not actually present. Two strong and experienced 'spirit release' mediums sit together, and the past life consciousness speaks through the yin sensitive, to be confronted by the yang partner who needs some ability in clairvoyance or clairsentience to be fully alert to what is happening.

Many earlier lives who have committed dreadful acts and have faced up to this in the spirit realms, find that when they come down close to the Earth atmosphere their former natures take over. They lie and pretend to be what they are not. The yang sensitive must be aware of any deceptions and must be able to challenge and confront their devious posturing or false humility while, at the same time, encouraging them to consider the benefits that will come if an honest approach is taken. This sensitive needs to be both firm and compassionate, both focused and optimistic, or these discarnate ones will get away with their prevarications.

**Mental Illness**
Karma is one of the main concerns of this life, to redress a balance without falling back into earlier behaviour. This requires you to deal with the pressure built up by former lives, who are still grappling ineffectively with the energies aroused. By focusing your intention deep into the heart, beyond any past limitations, you can discover more productive ways of dealing with the situation.

A working relationship with each past life needs to be developed subliminally, with both minds providing enough determination to carry it through. Even when they can't, you must. Keep focusing, keep allowing, and hold on to your faith. Then, out of the unravelling of the twisted energies that have, for so long, been suppressing your instinct for conclusive action, blockages will be dissolved and whole areas of your life remade.

But some people are lazy, shiftless and indulgent. At school, they do not stick to their lessons, do not train their minds at all or engage in any kind of moral discipline that would enable them to be still and strong in dealing with the energy distortions inherited from a former life that are still undermining the present. They allow all kinds of foolish attitudes to remain active in the subconscious mind.

Any past lives, fully prepared for their particular out-working, will see no advantage in coming forward into this unpromising situation. They have to rely on the discipline of the human participant to effect change and they know that nothing can be achieved with the present life in that state. So, they keep their distance and the least ready ones venture down close, only to reawaken the negative states from their past, so strongly, that they are overwhelmed by the force of what had been, and it will be a case of one leading the other into further misadventures and confusion.

Mental illness is often caused by a belligerent earlier life invading an undisciplined present one, but the mind imposing itself does not have to be part of the destiny plan. Very often it is one of those lives who were rejected or did not bother to come forward in the Hall of Incarnations, and these aggressive, manipulative, ego-centred kinds of individuals can take advantage when the human host is particularly weak willed.

If you approach someone sprawled out drunk on the pavement, you can actually talk to a past life. The ranting and anger clearly isn't coming from the one lying there. Whenever there is a severe character defect, a way can be opened up through drug taking, or the loss of a loved one, or a great shock to the system, but usually, it is a gradual thing—the past personality influencing the present one for a while before taking advantage of a breach in the aura to effectively take over.

Then there are mental conditions such as schizophrenia where a past personality projects its presence so strongly that the incumbent mind is compromised. There may be a number of past lives involved but usually one will be the ringleader. Before long, the past personality is directing the present one along inappropriate paths, with irrational ideas dominating. This is not to say that all schizophrenia is caused by this, but it is a fairly common situation for a weak, indecisive sort of person to be forcefully encroached on by past lives of theirs who have not much understanding but they still like to be in control. This can be an exceedingly difficult state to resolve.

## The Breakthrough Life

These then, are the issues of our time. Destructive karma of a most virulent kind is rampant across the world. The energy from all of your still-defiant lives, representing the lowest parts of your source nature, are linking up with many others to create a crisis for the planet. So, stop and make contact with your positive lives, some of whom have banded together to send you waves of encouragement from a higher level.

Are you aware of their support? Are you inviting their power down to counteract the negative streams of thought from your more wayward former lives? They aren't in the destiny chart for your life and they don't need to be, but they are nevertheless maintaining a shield of protection around you, keeping out some of the most corrupt shadow influences that are holding down the ego-bound masses today.

It is imperative to harness the power that they're making available to you, but do realise that streams of higher consciousness can only penetrate to the extent that you reach towards them. These are your true supporters and they need to become the dominant influence for your life. This is the perfect time for this to happen, to release the energies from the lesser lives by not encouraging their lowering influences to intrude too much. As you link into that special space in your heart, the good and pure can slip through, lifting you towards a much more profound sensitivity; then, you will begin to realise your most substantial aspirations.

The build-up of the Aquarian energies has given many people the opportunity to move beyond the harsh ways of the past once and for all. I trust that you are one of these. There are four occasions granted during every life when you can step off your own wheel of karma completely, and this current period will most likely provide one of them.

## Your Final Test

So, let's go through a progression of lives and see how the remaining karmic energies appropriate to this life, can finally be resolved. Imagine this is you even if the details don't fit. We will presume you had a very insensitive male incarnation way back who behaved with callous disregard for the needs and feelings of others. When you were in the womb, this time, the former energies reached out through your etheric consciousness into the world around and attracted responses that subtly influenced your developing sub-conscious mind.

As a child, your father's insensitivity and the harsh treatment of your mother—the outbursts of anger, the rejection of her worth—impacted severely on your young mind. As you still had a strong empathetic attachment to her, your soul was, in a sense, a magnet drawing these energies to you. Your siblings were not so deeply affected. The outer reality reflects the inner, and deep down, your soul knew how to make use of this. So, as a child you had the choice—either accept this abusive behaviour or become numb to it.

You became the antithesis of your father on the surface, though underneath, a harsh tendency has been there all along. It had built up over a number of lives, not with excessive malice or cruelty in the early days, for back then it was an instinctive energy. You had developed a strong wish to nurture those close to you, but a bitter, defensive mistrust of those you felt might do you harm was directed irrationally into many situations. This is understandable, for those were primitive times centred around personal survival. It was not understood that you attract what you fear.

The conscience wasn't very strongly developed back then either and so it was of little consequence if strangers were harmed in this battle for survival. However, guilt was aroused when one particular life was not strong enough to protect his immediate family. Other male members of the tribe were more effective providers and, therefore, more respected. The shame that accompanied this led him to reject the gods, and this obscured his direct connection to the Divine Father.

This alienation was felt again in the next life, when the other siblings got more than their share of the parental attention. So, resentment built up over a whole series of lives, particularly one in a deformed female body. The feelings of inadequacy peaked at that time and she never married. She lived alone in a small cottage at the edge of the village, and people thought she might be a witch.

Now, in a later male incarnation as an influential priest in the Catholic Church, he expressed his masculinity in very over-bearing ways. He treated all women as inferior, and while he was careful to exhibit the expected caring qualities in his parish duties, this was certainly not extended towards those he saw as rivals. As a consequence, he developed some rather heartless tendencies and was able to manoeuvre himself into the position of bishop. From there, he managed to wield considerable power within the church hierarchy, and he dealt ruthlessly with anyone who challenged his position and beliefs, which were narrow in the extreme. He behaved like so many men do in positions of power today. The appetite for intrigue grew even stronger and debased everything he came in contact with. But the pope remained oblivious to his web of deceit and double dealing.

After this self-serving incarnation, he returned to the astral world and relived all the harsh experiences as an essential part of the purging process that released him fully into the heavenly world. He realised that he had developed an energy over which his spirit had little influence, and had allowed attitudes that were clearly not in harmony with his divine purpose to find unfettered expression. It was obvious that these matters would have to be addressed, for this exaggerated dark side was denying him the scintillating rays of colour that are available on the pure mental planes.

These indescribable hues, fusions of spirit and creative purpose, are of such potency and variety, that a vibrancy could be weaved into his thoughts, lifting him into a glorious transcended reality, if only he were open to them. Alas, they were far out of range and he was held down by the shadow elements that continued to invade his soul. He enthusiastically followed the attractions of the dark ways in the spirit world as he had on Earth, and he remained unrepentant.

There are periods when relentlessly exploring the shadow side is an essential part of self discovery. These phases can extend over hundreds of years and many lives. There was even one instance where a most recent life was not chosen to plan the next. There just wasn't the sensitivity, and the others convinced the Lords of Karma to overlook him, so that a far more compassionate incarnation could be generated. In a sense, he put himself out of the loop.

Many times, an anguished cry came from the depths of his soul, a desperate plea to be released from the relentless pain that had built up. It seemed never ending but, at last, a desolation of such intensity marked the nadir of his soul's separation from its Maker and, for the first time, it was possible for him to look deeply into his heart for a way out. Then came a brief flash of the joys that would come in a full reunion with his Divine Nature, and it was time to start the long journey home.

All of the lives we are considering needed to continually access the inner light of spirit to strengthen them when they meet up on the astral plane with many of the people they have harmed. Several chose to come close to the Earth to work around groups of religious people promoting conflict and there were plenty of opportunities for this over the centuries. When they succeeded in preventing the butchery, a store of compassion and resolve was built up in the ethers that could be drawn on later.

Several more lives of this kind were necessary before the soul reached the point where it could be lifted onto a higher plane of existence. Overall, hundreds of years had passed, and the time had come for the next seed essence to be given its chance to achieve this transformation. In the planning for this life, some the most debased of the remaining issues were included in the destiny pattern to be worked on stage by stage.

Occasionally, the shining rays of spirit had penetrated glimpses of what would become possible later. This eased some of the pain, but the way to achieve any lasting relief was still blocked by the heaviness of those things from the wild, undisciplined earlier days on Earth. And here you are now, having passed through that ghastly time as a child in an abusive family situation where you felt so abandoned by God.

Various reconciliations have been effected in the spirit world, but the gains have not yet been realised within the physical experience. The light that you opened up to as you were born has since been blocked by the dark cloud that formed as you progressed through the various preparatory stages in your life. This cloud is totally illusory, for the light is there in its fullness and you have earned the right to it.

Soon you will break through, here and there, and flashes of illumination will be directed into your heart, and there will be short periods of respite from the struggle. You have reached a point in your evolution where you have resolved the most serious inner conflicts. You have a fairly balanced life, as a healer and a teacher. Nevertheless, you feel that you have been only partially successful in dealing with your most resistant issues. You have been a fairly effective parent, you are reasonably honest in your financial dealings, you are quite a good listener, and you are willing to help out when asked by someone you care for. But the higher forms of love still elude you.

However, this ordinariness masks the actual progress you are making towards embodying the more substantial state of being that is building up behind the scenes. The time is fast approaching when you will have sufficient soul maturity to face your remaining shadow elements in their last ditch stand. You must be especially vigilant as you pass through the devilishly difficult wilderness period. You will have the chance to transcend these dark compulsions by facing the temptation to succumb to the most virulent forms of your old behaviour, and then you must arouse your divine nature so that you can step beyond them entirely. This has to be negotiated very carefully; you can't rush it.

The past lifetimes will come forward in pairs, one of the most malevolent of your lives with one of the most elevated, one masculine, one feminine, to establish a balance between the yin and the yang elements.

The penultimate confrontation between the polarised light and dark elements within you will enable you to break down all resistance to the essential co-operation that must be sustained during the final stage of purification. This also requires you to extend unconditional love to those who will approach you for help in facing their inner demons. Your intervention will arouse their own inner healer to its highest degree, bringing freedom to the suppressed energies held tight inside the cancer or behind the confused state of mind.

The call to high service requires all your abilities to be activated, your ingenuity to be sharpened, for the shadow is, at this refined level, immensely determined to outwit you by undermining those you have been inspired to help, and will be looking for a way in.

To serve the planet in the ultimate way requires you to go beyond all judgement, reaching towards the light and the dark impartially. As you gradually become whole, you help others to become whole. Their struggles, their feelings of desolation, their separation from God, must ignite an immense compassion within you. Only then will the remaining wisps of your dark cloud clear, and liberated waves will pulse out to the ends of your universe. This is the breakthrough moment you have been waiting for over aeons of time when, at last, the great Creative Spirit and Gaia's domain become one within your heart, and you are complete.

# 12
# Global Karma

**Transformation of the Universe**
The progress of each planet is closely linked to the destinies of all the others. If Saturn was to move too far ahead in evolution, this would increase the pressures and challenges that Earth must face; rather like when a country gets too powerful, precipitating a state of tension that upsets the integrity and stability of its neighbours.

Likewise, the life of the planet is an intricate co-operation between all the manifest life forms on it and within it, that needs to develop in harmony with the universal plan. It is a finely balanced environment we live in and we have incarnated with a responsibility not only to our own progression, but also to participate in the global karma being outworked around us, and from which we can never be separate.

From the higher planes, human evolution is managed through the procession of the seasons, rather than day to day events. And in the realms of the angels, where harmony has already been secured by the legions of light, progress is viewed in decades rather than years. However, humankind is still battling through the crippling echoes of negative energy from the past, and we are not going to bring down this triumph over the divisive shadow forces into physical manifestation all that readily.

The higher beings cannot overrule free will, they can only use what has already been generated on Earth. I have mentioned the banks of constructive power that are built up in the ethers. There are many dreadful things being done to the planet today that could be prevented by drawing on these banks, but in most instances, humankind has to be allowed to make its mistakes, for once this power is used, it is no longer available.

There are also accumulations of twisted retrograde power being used to fuel the movements and conflicts dragging humanity down into even greater degradation. The shadow band believe that if they can prevent light getting into the minds of those in positions of authority, we will not be able to reverse the decline in time. However, their stock of perverse power is gradually being depleted and their period of global dominance will come to an end. How long will that take? I am aware of no current guidance offering enlightenment on this. We will just have to wait and see how it unfolds.

**Planetary Chaos**
The residues of karma that lie in each of us, are encouraging a worldwide outbreak of indecision and fear, interspersed with aggressive, precipitous action. Unwitting allegiance to the shadow is causing governments to allow, even encourage, the destruction of the natural order in the name of progress. In the global arena, this irresponsible behaviour has barely been challenged.

It is not surprising that many leaders are addicted to the old forms of manipulation; very rigid patterns of belief have been built up over hundreds of years in parliament and in the court houses and these are influencing the present incumbents. There are those past leaders on the astral plane who are helping to defend these institutions against the energies of change that will bring about a root and branch conversion.

Church leaders are likewise surrounded and hampered by those on the inner levels who preceded them, those who are still bound within the very tight religious structures they helped create when on Earth. They have accepted what they believe is a god-appointed responsibility to keep their ideologies intact. It happens in all institutions that have achieved some measure of longevity, which includes the Theosophists, the Anthroposophists and the Quakers. Attempts to effect reform are being blocked by the hierarchy of souls on the astral level, along with a few on the mental level, who are preventing progressive ideas coming in from above

Many of the political hierarchy on the astral plane cannot even contemplate a situation where they are not in charge and able to inflict their misguided attitudes onto human affairs. They have little difficulty in recruiting hoards of conservatives in physical form to join them. They are the diehards, the purists, the bullies who are working to polarise public support as they always did. And it is the actions and inaction of the incarnate ones held in their thrall that is undermining the planetary well-being so disastrously.

This global mayhem is increasing the karmic build-up, and by dismissing and ridiculing rational alternatives, our leaders and their influential supporters are weaving more and more complications into our lives. We are caught, in a sense, between worlds and between ages, and by continuing to resist change, we can expect the disastrous climactic and physical disasters to continue. This is not in Earth's destiny plan; we are encouraging it through our stubborn refusal to confront the issues head-on that will bring about the much needed renewal.

Planetary expansion and contraction allows in waves of subtly motivated forms of energy. But this isn't enough for us; we are greedy for experience and our buzzy technological advances, and in the spiritual area we are obsessed with what appear to be higher realities but are actually creations of the shadow ones.

We human beings always want to be participating in really important events. We want it to be happening now, in our present life, under our control; we are not prepared to wait. "The Maitreya is here," one person proclaims. "Extra terrestrials are in our midst," says another, and that old chestnut, "The end of the world is nigh!" has found a new urgency. Instead, we must align ourselves entirely with the current needs of our planet, as servants to its unfoldment, not as its masters.

**Beneath the Surface**
When you look at world events you will notice that a conflict breaks out in one area for a time, then subsides. Soon after, disruption flares up in another country. It is almost as though someone is pulling strings. If everything happened at once, there would be chaos, so it is regulated by, what you could call, the Lords of International Karma.

We have to go right back, beyond recorded history, to find the beginnings of many of the conflicts erupting on the planet today. The Earth is a living being and there are power points all over it, rather like the acupuncture points found on the human body, and there are energy lines that link them up. Things carried out in one place can be transmitted to another and released through events happening there.

A group of souls who created negative karma in one country can later reincarnate elsewhere bringing that karma with them. For example, the treatment meted out by the church during the Spanish Inquisition, was of the most grotesque kind. Taking this forward to more recent times, some of these priests and politicians on the inner planes were looking around for a place to work this karma out. Spain no longer provided the right environment for this.

The Franco period had added a different layer of impacted energy that lay closer to the surface making the religious karma largely inaccessible. So, Northern Ireland was chosen by them as an appropriate destination.

In Ireland, sectarian conflicts have raged since time immemorial, and these disputes were added to by each succeeding generation until there was a bank of twisted power in place that would inspire any fanatic who tuned into it. With so much religious intolerance in the atmosphere, there could be no better place to face many of the issues left unresolved from the Inquisition. So, a large number of the priests and heretics and their followers from that earlier time decided to extend new incarnations into the Irish atmosphere to continue where they had left off.

The Irish situation had become an intractable conflict, with two distinct energies that needed to find ways of working together, with the differences celebrated, not opposed. The resolution of the religious issues there will make the Spanish reunification easier when the time for that comes. Ireland is a stepping stone towards this.

Remember that there is national karma and there is individual karma, and while these can be mutually interactive, they are not one and the same. I have indicated that specific areas on the planet are the equivalent of soul projections from its source mind, and the current boundaries of some countries do not coincide with the true spiritual divisions required. This is the cause of the unrest being stirred up in Iraq, a country thrown together by Western nations for their convenience, or in specific ethnic areas within countries such as Tibet, precariously positioned within China. All around the world, there are breakaway groups, some of them legitimate, and others, totally misguided.

Even when the boundaries of a country are reasonably accurate, there may be two or more separate group souls operating there which have completely different ideas on how the country should progress, and these are at loggerheads. The Basque and Catalan separatist movements reflect karma from two quite different historical periods of subjugation, and remain dangerous strands of the Spanish destiny that must be addressed and integrated, not marginalised and suppressed. The Catholic Church there will have its inevitable 'make or break' crisis a little further down the line.

## The Earth Conceives

Does the planet have a soul and a set of bodies as we do? Most definitely! Over the past 100 or so years, the next division of the global source mind has been projecting a specific, finely tuned destiny progression into the soul of the planet. This completely new concentration of enhanced purpose has been blended into the etheric consciousness as a many-layered energy that covers the full Aquarian span.

This dispensation not only surrounds us and sets into place the new forms and directions that humanity needs, it resonates right through to engage the various inhabitants of inner Earth working under the jurisdiction of Gaia who need to anchor these energies on the surface of the planet from inside, in much the same way that we do from outside it.

If balance is to return through our mutual efforts, then we on the surface must draw on the etheric enhancement building up in the atmosphere surrounding the Earth as they must receive inspiration from deep within it, so that our way can be nurtured and enlivened in harmony with theirs.

The Aquarian nature is currently descending as an integrated multi-dimensional reality needing to be brought into harmony with the residues of the past, but it is far from complete. While many people are embracing the liberated nature of the mind orientated Aquarian energy and have cast off many outworn and misguided attitudes, in their haste, they are unwisely ignoring or rejecting many worthwhile continuations of the Piscean energy.

The Piscean age was meant to provide a masculine outer presence with the sensitive feminine Piscean nature shining strongly through. And now, it is the authority of the feminine element that needs to be there in front, but with the mentally inquisitive Aquarian tendency projecting through from within.

The generous and non-judgemental nature of Pisces has been restrained over the past two thousand years. When the ever-trusting Piscean energy did try to assert itself, the dominant outer presence felt threatened, fearing that its authority would be diminished by it. So, an aggressive, controlling force was unleashed to suppress everything it perceived as sensitive and weak. Strict tribal loyalties enabled extremely repressive systems of governance and belief to be set up. In a sense, an alien nature was inflicted on the entire age.

We have seen the feminine shut out during the Piscean age, and there is a danger that the masculine will be similarly denied in the Aquarian age. It is a definite possibility if we don't find harmony and balance within ourselves very soon.

At a time when wars can be fought with devastating effect, leaders are still slow in realising that force is counter-productive. Peaceful solutions seem as far off as ever, yet the emerging Aquarian energies are gradually breaking up these loyalties, bringing about an independence of thought that will make a real difference.

The transformative power of this coming Aquarian age will cast off the shackles of the past for those people who are ready for new heights of awareness. The awakening that follows must be used to unravel the awful energy constructions that many others still remain locked into.

The balance of the Earth has been unsettled, pulled right away from its true state by the higher ones attempting to move evolution forward. This is being resisted by the shadow clans who wish to continue their dominance over the Earth. Eventually, circumstances will compel them to let go of their control, and the force of it will spring back onto us all. Provided sufficient numbers of people have developed themselves as crucibles of change, much of the remaining karmic energy will then be taken in and transformed. Only then will the pendulum swing free again, heralding, energising and, then, manifesting the harmonious future for the planet that has been predicted by the sages of old.

That is the optimistic progression of events. A surge back through the past, chronologically 'sucking up' the remaining bits of karma is urgently needed because the legacy left by the various imperialist empires that prospered over the past two thousand years needs to be fully addressed, particularly in England.

**A view ahead**

We will now look more closely at the matter of group karma and at the paths, some stretching far back into earlier periods of unresolved turbulence, that have led us to this present global crisis. People want to know what the future holds, as if by this knowledge alone they can better negotiate the tortuous path that will see them through it. The scriptures tell us of the time when the lion will be at one with the lamb, and many people working on a wavelength of prayer and meditation are sensing something of the future perfection though it is, as yet, a mere blueprint in the ethers. Higher consciousness is not automatically brought down. Without some understanding of how the ways to this perfection are blocked, and unless there is a willingness to engage in the removal of these restrictions, it will remain out of reach.

All of our hapless politicians, lurching from one confrontation to another, one crisis to another, unable to admit to the real motives behind their systems of control and lack of trust who, despite their professed willingness to respond to the wishes of the people, still settle for short-term advantage.

In the last century, two world wars, countless other conflicts, regular recessions, economic bubbles bursting unexpectedly, and galloping inflation have pulled the rug from under the securities that many cling to. But while all of these provided our leaders with opportunities to learn lessons, greed caused them to forget the reasons for controls existing; now their systems are being tested to the limit, once again.

Clearly, if humankind is to survive intact in these increasingly uncertain times, it is important to embrace the unexpected. Equally, by sensing something of what lies ahead and altering the misguided approaches that are preventing more favourable opportunities being drawn forward, we will be able to gradually erect strong foundations for the future that will withstand the buffeting of the winds of chance and change.

Our very human, but misguided determination, to evolve spiritually without a willingness to modify our acquisitive behaviour patterns, for reasons always based in fear, is placing great pressure on certain weak points in the Earth's aura and the future patterns are not being allowed to emerge securely.

In recent times, the forces of fire, tempest, and flooding have inflicted their might on many places on the globe, but these are merely the twinges. There are clearly major issues to be addressed or worse will follow. Uncommon levels of global cooperation, and considerable self-sacrifice are needed to heal the planetary wounds. To understand this, look at the human form. When the inner pressures begin to get too much, certain physical breakdowns begin to happen—colds, minor accidents, skin rashes, aches and pains and so on. There will always be warnings in the early stages, a sense of something not being right in a localised part of the body. The emotional life should be looked to as a possible source of disharmony, as well as the challenges to physical well-being caused by air, water and soil pollution.

If the self-destructive states of mind and behaviour continue, serious illnesses will ensue. The physical body is very astute, it always focuses on one part of itself in order to avert a complete breakdown—a kidney is lost, a heart attack lays the person aside for a time from some stressful situation. The more willing a person is to face the inner issues, the more easily they can be drawn to the surface and released without long-term damage. It is only when people bury their jealousy, their envy, and their hatred deep inside that the inoperable cancers occur. Your body will always do its best by you, so that you will be left, after a breakdown, in the best possible place to continue with the life ahead.

When extended out to the planetary body, the seat of the cause and the site of a malfunction may also be in different places. There are complementary links within any life form, and so some of the negative energies from conflicts out of control in one place are being channelled to other spots that are mature enough spiritually to deal with them. These places are bearing the brunt because of their particular relationship to the whole as chosen centres of transmutation. And, as the transforming power operates, so the healing power will come in.

Individuals who wish to relieve the pressure on all such special places are joining group endeavours, and these groups are linking up to their counterparts on the inner levels, so that, by engaging the affinities place to place, the power can flow through to assist. Any disharmony should be viewed as a sign that greater focus and direction must be applied to strengthen the links, and above all, a more subtle attunement is needed to the spheres of light, so that humankind may move cooperatively towards the anticipated time of 'Peace on Earth'. How smooth the transition will be is entirely up to us.

**Into Aquarius**
Many people, sensitive to the energies of change entering our atmosphere linked to the changeover of Pisces into Aquarius, are aware that humanity is being offered the chance to receive a massive upliftment and they are expecting exceptional things to come from it. However, their view of this period often involves a physical transformation; however, I believe that these rapidly emerging energies are being focussed primarily at the etheric body

of Earth, not its physical counterpart.

Consider your own moment of conception. It was a momentous event for the incoming soul, but for your mother it may well have passed un-noticed. The human form takes time to grow into its new existence. It is the nine months in the womb where the planned components of the physical body come together. Only then can it emerge as an independent physical entity. The karmic constraints set up by homo sapiens during the Piscean age are not part of the Aquarian destiny but will nevertheless greatly restrict our ability to respond to the issues facing the planet as it becomes imbued with its new responsibilities. This will most likely prevent any heightened expression gathering strength in the material world for quite a while.

The physical body doesn't burst out fully formed at the time of conception and neither will a rejuvenated physical Earth. This time of transformation can be viewed as a sudden merging of some much more refined streams of potential into the etheric body of Earth, right through to its core. It will require a massive adjustment and any upheavals in the physical world such as earthquakes, hurricanes, and tsunamis, will be due to reactions by Gaia to these enhanced energies flowing in. She is responding with bursts and eruptions of exasperation as she struggles to keep her newly invigorated self in balance.

Consequently, from the moment of 'conception' for the Aquarian age, we will be busy grappling with our own and the Earth's backlog of karma and, instead of experiencing this significant event as a harmonious transition, it will be hidden behind the turmoil of our present economic and ecological challenges. It will be a long while before the etheric energies, imbued with an Aquarian purpose, are ready to fully engage in physical expression, hopefully with the Piscean karma finally removed; even then, it will be a baby Aquarius we are relating to.

Ultimately it comes down to our own individual connection with the guidance from our spirit consciousness as to whether we will negotiate the rapid changes in the way we need to, by loving each other and the planet unconditionally.

## The Thirteenth Life

We incarnate in many different countries over a full cycle in order to gain a wide ranging set of experiences and to grow in complexity through absorbing the archetypal energy that each provides. We are involved in one for a time before moving on to another but, where karma is incurred, some countries will be returned to at a later date. There are many and diverse experiences to be had under the influence of national archetypes and within the racial archetypes, religious archetypes, and vocational archetypes. There are so many that need to be introduced and assimilated over time.

I have pointed out that a cycle of human incarnations tends to be twelve, but there is a thirteenth life that invariably follows each set. This is often designed to coincide with a very special influx of energy onto the planet. Many people had a thirteenth life at the time Jesus was on the Earth. His main mission was to put designs and objectives into place in the ethers, far-reaching energies of transformation that could not find expression in human activity at that time. He was the avatar for the Aquarian age, not the Piscean.

We will have to wait a while longer as we collectively work through the remaining critical surges of karma that will continue to challenge us for generations to come. When the time is ripe, and that will not be until the next century, a significantly heightened emergence of the Christ energy will occur in our midst. It will be truly magnificent when experienced in its divine simplicity. At that time, many spirit families will incarnate together to carry out some very special mission, such as to run a country in keeping with higher principles. And, many of the people involved will be having a thirteenth life.

It will first show itself in the Middle East, with the emergence of the first of twelve leaders of considerable spiritual stature who will together integrate the energies of the great Christ spirit into the ways of humanity, spreading unconditional love to every part of the globe. The avatar energy this time will be through twelve, with the thirteenth, the Jesus oversoul focussed down into a high etheric orientation. Only the most elevated of souls incarnate at that time will be able to reach up to him directly.

For a future life of ours to be one of those who participate at that level, we will need to have gradually developed the ability to channel some of these powerful energies of the higher planes, steeped in the ways of unification. We are preparing for that time when we must respond to world events from deep within us, so that these new world teachers will find a welcome, not martyrdom, this time around.

When the statement of the Master Jesus, "I am the way, the truth, and the life, and no man comes unto the Father except by me," is stripped of the pride that seems to be there, we can see that all of us are walking and living our lives here on Earth so that the power of redemption can be with us and can operate through us.

**The Way of Redemption**
As the Aquarian Age takes over, there will be a culmination in the process of release that has been so evident in recent times, when all the accumulated bile of the past is discharged into the Earth atmosphere. To meet this challenge, an increasing number of people are stirring that spiritual part of themselves, but in doing so, they may well be shocked by what they see and feel as they become more sensitive to the mounting harshness of the world around them. The next few years will be a very precarious time for anyone opening up to an elevated perspective for the first time.

Already, many are so concerned with their own spiritual development, that they deny the need to share this as part of their commitment. Some people who sit regularly in meditation, are beginning to go blind or deaf rather than participate in the outer world they find so abhorrent. Others remain surrounded by people of like mind, trying to reach out towards a perfection that is further off in the scheme of evolution than they are willing to recognise.

Many today are seeking transcendental states which will only leave them befuddled and uncertain, out of touch with the physical reality that they have come onto this Earth to progress. They become isolated in the locked room of their own or a collective mind, reaching up to the power and love of spirit and drawing it down into them where it begins to run amok within the personality in a vain attempt to find expression.

To gain anything lasting in a spiritual sense, people have to build upon experience, upon past mistakes, and respond to the call of service that is to be expressed through them.

Those who lead the way have a massive responsibility to inspire humanity as the Masters did. But even here, while recognising their personal and group responsibility, some do not like to get their hands dirty. They inhabit a spiritual enclave, often feeling they have a divine task to promulgate a vision of a new order, but do not reach out in any practical way to those facing, and often losing, the uphill battle right now in those places of darkness and oppression.

All true world servers must be willing to be inwardly led into many environments where they would not normally choose to go—into a revivalist spiritual meeting where the emotions run riot; into places where mind-expanding drugs are taken and a rock group is belting out songs of a quasi-spiritual nature, to be surrounded by young people whose way of life is quite alien to their own and quite removed from any kind of spiritual practice. Yet, they find themselves there.

And, if you could see what is happening on the inner planes, you would be aware that many of these young people have been lifted up, almost against their will, into contact with a larger light. Many who walked with the Master Jesus, are there working, getting closer to these people as they open up in a very emotional way to something that lifts their hearts high. Oh, they will be let down once the concert is over, but for a short time they have been living in a borrowed light. They will have gained something that will reveal itself more fully when they have progressed a little further along the path.

Many who came into contact with Jesus, who were at the time unable to appreciate or make use of what they received, are now working through a current incarnation. They are conscious that it is through this contact that they are now able to tread the path more securely. Jesus went among the vagrants and money lenders, for surely the way has got to be opened up for them and someone has to stand at the door. There is no task that the great Masters undertook that their followers should shirk from doing.

If people of spiritual understanding were not present at those rock concerts, very little could be achieved. There are these things, emanating from below, that have, because of man's atrocities and misdeeds throughout the ages, been buried deep in the Earth, and they must now be allowed to rise up in places where people are at their most open and receptive. But it must first pass through a human channel who is able to take in some of these subterranean wrongs and transform the energy within them into a light that can be borrowed by those in need who have gathered around, or the unsuitable power will swamp the atmosphere once again.

Only the Earth can redeem the Earth. The higher rays, though directed where they are needed by the stewards of spirit, cannot penetrate very deeply into the being of humankind, into the hearts and minds of the men and women who are experiencing a tentative awakening, except that the stewards of Earth are active with them, taking their particular manifestation of light into the darkest places, into the ghettos, among the sick and the poor and the lost, and into places where power has been misused in the past or is still being misused, as they become strong enough to do so.

No level of humanity can be excluded from the process. Servants of the way must go where they are led. Each must bring down as much light as they can handle, with the heavy Earth power lifted up to meet it in the solar plexus crucible of their being, to be transmuted, and that refinement passed out to the world in love. This surely is the way of redemption.

# 13
# The Quickening

**Karma escalates**
In the early days, a kind of balance was achieved by couples, the man hunted for food and the wife cooked it. This clear separation of responsibility worked quite well. A whole lifetime was spent in one of these roles, and then the other was experienced in a later incarnation. You were rich and then you experienced a life of extreme poverty. You were a land owner with many slaves in one incarnation, and a slave in another to learn what it's like to be on the receiving end.

These ways of moving towards wisdom and overall harmony, snake through time as people choose to experience alternate polarities, though not necessarily in the following incarnation. The complementary experience may come three lifetimes later because it will often take a lot of inner plane work before it is appropriate to attempt a major balancing initiative in the harsh human arena, but balance must eventually come.

At this crucial point, when everything is speeding up, people are trying to harmonise many things within a single lifetime, weaving backwards and forwards, the yin and the yang expressed in quite different contexts, balancing the soul in a much more immediate and comprehensive manner. They are outgoing for a time and very reclusive later on. They try Buddhism, which expresses the yin ventricle of the heart, and then Christianity which is the yang. Then they leave religion altogether for an alternative lifestyle rooted in a pagan past and linking the mystical to the earth. Nothing is new, really. These spiralling opportunities return out of the mists of time to throw up complexities that demand far more of us each time round.

We can't just live through routine, we have to extend ourselves, take risks, and by letting go of our herd nature, we discover our own particular brand of truth that always resides near to a precise balance point; it can exist nowhere else.

Now, you could say, "If I walked down Buddha's 'middle way', I wouldn't really be living a normal life, would I?" and that is true. To live through detachment is a strange experience at first. Though you don't actually walk down the centre, you do reach a state like breathing, oscillating backwards and forwards between two complementary experiences in a very gentle, natural way.

Held between the male and female principles, between the past and future, and between heaven and Earth, you can flow through life exploring the inner and outer extent of your chosen experience in a very personal, sensitively regulated manner, without much indecision or conflict. The point of inner stillness draws the outer edges of human nature into a swirl of perpetual rejuvenation.

Disturbance will inevitably go on around you, but you can balance the extremes. You don't take sides nor do you buy into any conflict because you know that you'll always be the loser if you do. Your personal beliefs are never imposed on others; you have learned the ways of true intimacy by allowing your divine nature, your unique qualities, to shine through without eclipsing the divinity in others.

You have discovered an immediacy, yet there is all the time in the world to reach your destination. You are serenely treading a balanced path between the two poles, never getting involved in any of the dramatic love-hate relationships that people so often choose. If you continue the polarised attitudes and responses of earlier lifetimes you will more confidently create havoc in later ones.

**Paradox Reigns**
We humans are such contradictory creatures. Many people, with apparently sound motives, are hiding rather irresponsible inclinations and they get caught up in all sorts of moral dilemmas when facing the unresolved issues in themselves. Doctors have to adhere to spiritual law in very tricky ethical situations—abortion is one of these, as is euthanasia. Judges are required to uphold laws that they

do not personally believe in. Politicians with a strong religious faith are confronted by many tough decisions when humility is lacking. Their high ethical position is undermined by an ego fuelled impatience, or a strong need for approval, and they are unable to resolve their duplicity without compromising their image and their prospects.

They often turn from good intentions to the same old shifty behaviour that inevitably leads to even more inequality, and then they slip and slide around trying to justify their actions. Compromise, allied to self interest, turns to downright moral capitulation. They are representing us as we were, not as we need to be now, and they get away with it because most of us are personally caught up in exactly the same dilemmas. Who are we to cast the first stone? Wherever fear is, you can be sure that the shadow has been aroused and a couple of wily past personalities lurking in the background are intruding their own wayward tendencies while, at the same time, secretly willing us to go beyond their manipulations.

Spiritually orientated people are finding that affirmative action within a world that does not share their high principles is very difficult, for every step demands greater awareness and courage. A genuine moral crusader will be confronted by those who have taken on the role of antagonist—people locked into old polarised attitudes, who are still unable to reconcile the ethical conflicts aroused within themselves. They relentlessly assert their warped values into every situation. These ones need to have their soul immaturity exposed to the light of truth. Only then will they find the humility to step down gracefully.

In some countries, an aura of national superiority is undermined by its reverse, inadequacy mired in repressed guilt, which is often caused by the privileged elite not having done enough to help the dispossessed and downtrodden. It is particularly severe in those countries where the white majority have completely failed their indigenous populations, such as in Australia and the USA. Governments which can't face the consequences of their actions in their own backyard, may relieve their guilt by directing controlling inclinations farther afield. It came to a head in 9/11 and was displaced into the Iraq war. The lessons still have not been learnt. Another crisis will inevitably burst onto the international stage, and this will go on, more and less severely, until the lesson of non-attachment has been properly learnt.

## The Opportunities Keep Coming

As I see it, it is already too late for humanity, overall, to reach up to the highest spiritual awakening that was available to us, although individuals can. In the ethers, a band of vibrant, transformative energy encircles the Earth. All that people have come to face and transcend is being drawn to the surface. It is a crash course in spiritual evolution we are involved in now. Spiritual seekers must quickly resolve a substantial portion of their individual karma so that they can soar to the heights. Opportunities like this don't come around all that often.

Peter and his disciple colleagues could have stood by their master in his time of need but they fell short, and Christianity was begun on a lower rung of achievement than it might have been. Already this new Aquarian age is being launched below its true capability. Humanity can only do what it is ready for. We will move forward at the highest level we can manage to achieve and sustain. The Earth will go on, whatever happens, but the quality of the future that can be enjoyed by homo sapiens is still gravely uncertain.

Many rich nations have produced leaders who were easily tricked by the shadow band into putting policies and procedures into place that would be enthusiastically supported or violently opposed by people of an extreme disposition but, in fact, it was masterminded from above them by more benevolent minds with a responsibility to bring a higher power into planetary affairs. It was their influence that was to lead those countries into extreme positions that would lead to a breakdown of the existing systems—a dramatic resolution was called for.

Of course, I am not condoning the hardship, oppression and loss of life that has occurred in the name of freedom in many places but, for blocks to be removed, it is sometimes necessary to allow the pendulum to be drawn even further away from its balance, so that the machinations of the power brokers of this world can be identified and their immense structures of deceit revealed.

Only then will ordinary people feel sufficiently aggrieved, sufficiently motivated in their hearts to utter a collective plea for leaders of stature to step into the limelight with a new, inclusive, life-enhancing approach to global affairs. "Enough is enough" is must continue to surge around the globe, sweeping from power those who cannot measure up. And then the pendulum can swing free and, in time, return to a stable position on a higher level of accomplishment.

This is what the world requires now, spiritually motivated people ready to step up to the plate of high office, but they will need to be sure that the necessary support for them is fully there, right through all strata of society, so that they can mobilise a global thrust of liberation that will last.

The moment has to be right for these men and women of peace to emerge. Many are already positioned out of the limelight, held back by our lack of readiness to fully throw our weight behind them. The plight of the Burmese monks, as they made their little push for freedom, clearly showed that, and we only have to look back to the life of Jesus to know that support may not be there when the really conclusive steps have to be taken.

The vast karmic influences affecting us, extensions of universal imbalance, are the primary cause of all global, national, and communal unease. If your individual karmic responsibility was to be broken down, seventy percent of it might be personal karma, with ten percent linked to the ancestral family you were born into, stretching back seven generations, ten percent coming from the community or country where your primary allegiance lies, and ten percent of it is the planetary karma.

At this time, group karma is being aroused in communities everywhere to such an alarming degree that the whole of civilisation is under threat and very strong antidotes are required. We want to be free of it, and a few on the spiritual fringes, are conjuring up grand scenarios of God intervening and saving them from the consequences of their past misdeeds. They expect to be dramatically lifted up onto a higher arc of experience where they will occupy favoured places in the hierarchy overseeing the planet. I suspect there will be no spontaneous ascension with chosen ones lifted up en masse into an elevated human consciousness. This is a fantasy perspective, but a nation of individuals promoting change can certainly make a difference.

**The New Morality**
A global awakening is most urgently needed, with each individual accessing a little more of the light within and a little more of the dark, and bringing these into a joyful reunion. Fifty percent of the power our leaders require to carry forward their mission needs to come from us. We must be willing to join them with our own demonstration of personal responsibility. Then they and we will realise that the Christ in the heavens and the Christ deep within every human heart are one and the same. Only then will the deceptive inducements and promises of the shadow band, lurking behind human affairs, cease to have any power.

All is not lost. A few of the new kind of leaders have already stepped forward and started to clear out the debris of the past, in this long, tortuous process of unifying the planet. These pioneers are demonstrating unremitting patience and courage in the face of intractable opposition. They are preparing the way for the ones to follow, who really will be able to inspire a much more humane, more balanced future into being on a global scale.

In country after country, exhilarating developments are happening, new voices are inspiring many to step out of the cage of their own past into the freedom that awaits them. Mass movements demanding change are growing in numbers. The waves of opportunity that we can ride high on, are mounting in strength; each one would catch your breath short with awe as you slide, arms outstretched, like an eagle soaring into the heavens.

It will not get any easier, but the opportunities will continue to come as the next uplifting surge, and the next, invite us to risk everything. Some intrepid ones are already mastering the energies that curl upwards carrying their balanced souls into heightened spiritual attainment. Maybe this is happening to you.

**Britannia Challenged**
There is national karma to work out everywhere, and some of this is not easy to fathom, particularly where it was set into motion in pre-historic times. As the Aquarian energies become stronger over the next few years, the global shadow forces will be even more starkly revealed. However, it only takes one country, where everything works exactly as its destiny requires, to inspire others. A look at the unfolding destiny of the planet reveals twelve phases to come, which are linked to the re-emergence of some of the great civilisations of the past in a new way, and the first of these will be England, commencing soon.

If you live in that country, you will be probably be aware of a heaviness in the atmosphere. There is a barrier to people extricating themselves from very restrictive conditions. The fortress mentality, so strongly present in this island state, is being aggravated because of a tremendous demand for support coming in from many places.

Countries have souls, and some of the more powerful of these are sub-divided and extended as paternal influences into other lands. For quite awhile now, Britain has felt restricted because of the backlash energies being drawn in from its imperialist past in many countries that it occupied and exploited—Pakistan, for example, and Zimbabwe where it left a particularly unsettled legacy. Some conflicted energies emanating from the present upheavals in these lands are being channelled into the English atmosphere, depleting the aura, and placing a tremendous pressure on the hearts of its people. The karma has certainly come home to roost.

Though there have been far worse occupying powers in the world, whatever is done to the people of any country that causes restriction and hardship will have to be worked out by succeeding generations who knew full well what they were getting into before they were born. This is included in their personal karma.

The English have the feeling that they need to isolate and defend themselves; this is always counter-productive. England has created a great deal of karma in the Middle East through many imperialist forays in times past. To invade a country in that region will arouse an already treacherous accumulation of resentment, with the inevitable repercussions.

You may not know that Sadam Hussein, in a former life, was one of those who put Jesus to death. Without such knowledge it is difficult to see him as anything other than a monster. But the great sense of unworthiness, that subsequently flooded through him, brought his soul into perpetual torment, a state so devastating that it eventually caused him to completely deny his involvement. So, with no adequate link to the past and no sense of inner responsibility for it, his soul became encrusted with ego and with that came a belligerent self-justification.

Through his Sadam persona and the position he held, all the appropriate elements were in place, not only to reveal the next phase of the destiny mapped out for Iraq, but also to arouse hidden grievances that would give many countries, rooted in a Christian heritage, the chance to discover unconditional love. And we have seen, through subsequent events, how far short of this ideal the Western alliance was to come. But that was the lesson that Jesus came to impart, a lesson that Sadam was much too arrogant to understand, and which was likewise not implemented by those who were to react so precipitously to him from outside Iraq, while claiming divine authority as a justification for their own harsh and unforgiving actions.

The culpability of England in this matter is far greater than America's because it is the more spiritually mature partner. It would have been wise for the British government to have listened to the vast number of its citizens opposed to the war, and taken the moral lead by being steadfast in the face of those resisting truly ethical change, on both sides. It must take that lead now. The powers of oppression in the world need a dogged determination and unwavering resilience to unseat them.

It is not easy to understand what is really behind the most dramatic things happening on the world scene, the full ramifications, because in this period of global re-unification, the legacy left behind by some of the past empires has grown into a monster version of itself, quite out of proportion to either historical precedent or present reality. Extreme forces just seem to rise up and take over.

## Planetary Karma to the Fore

A severe jolt to the Earth's aura many thousands of years ago resulted in a slight misalignment in the Earth axis and the baleful influence of the moon, that resulted, has intensified since. The Earth has a very uneasy relationship with its moon and it is lagging quite a bit behind some of the other planets in its evolutionary position. While human activity over the ages has added to the malaise, the basic imbalance of the Earth is the cause of this.

We are loathe to look deeply to understand how the current global unrest came about and why there is this tremendous alienation people feel from and for the planet that gives them life. We have diverted our attention to the surface of the Sun and to the surface of the planet, indeed, to the surface of most things. The surging heart of Earth is barely registered.

Near the surface, the elements are protesting, the fiery volcanoes, the natural gasses that we are rapidly depleting, and the water that we pollute in so many ways. A pressure has built up that will lead to even more global catastrophes if we don't heed the warnings.

Beneath this, Hades is there to remind us of our submerged shadow nature and, further down, we encounter the many wonders of the inner worlds, the crystal formations and the energy vortices that generate so much of the power that we benefit from on the surface. But we won't be able to enter the central area within the Earth which is completely non-physical. It resonates with the centre of the Sun, and the beings of light based there are working directly under Gaia.

Our Earth is a living being with its own levels of dark and light. But, these great forces are not in balance, causing us to feel very challenged much of the time. If the Earth were in a harmonious state, all life forms on it would automatically be at peace with each other.

We have stopped thanking the Earth for all the food and oxygen it provides us with, and this essentially reflects the Earth's attitude to itself. It is almost as if we are punishing the unbalanced Earth for arousing the undisciplined dark forces so strongly within us.

Those who created the original karma are under great pressure as the incoming energy quickens. Most members of the human community have allowed fear and self interest to take over and they support, openly or tacitly, the destructive initiatives that have been rampaging angrily across many lands, adding daily to the Earth's woes. But then, as I have said, the Earth is essentially responsible for everything that is happening to it. In addition, the denizens of inner Earth are trying to dampen down the effects of human activity that they do not find conducive. But, resisting what you don't like only amplifies it.

So, humanity is being held back by the planet's resistance to change within itself. The exaggeration of the masculine over the feminine in human behaviour came from the Earth's weakness in this regard. Gaia had allowed herself to be subdued and is now experiencing the consequences. Humanity and the Earth are interdependent, we have been together for a long time, and an injection of unconditional love from our senior partner would certainly help to spur us to become more respectful, inclusive and compassionate towards her and ourselves.

**The Insanity Escalates**

Many recent laws, designed to rescue a system in chaos, are taking even more power from the people they are intended to elevate. Everywhere, people are expressing outrage at our leaders who have no true vision, but few of us are making any practical commitment to doing anything about it. Those who ignore the contribution they could make in bringing people together must endure the terrible pain of separation.

Can we ever turn our backs on anything in the absolute confidence that this was not us at some former time, that we were not indirectly responsible for these divisive attitudes in evidence today that are at variance with planetary need? Can we hate anyone because of a different religion, or a different colour skin, when in all probability we once followed that religion and had that same colour skin?

When we weave compassion and goodwill into the fabric of the collective consciousness, each strand with its own colour and vibrancy, its own purpose and potency, we instil these qualities in ourselves. By linking our souls to the soul of the Earth, the great Creative Spirit can become alive within us.

Individuals have to move beyond the petty concerns of some of their former lives that have led them to self obsession and isolation. We need unity, not uniformity, in our dealings with many of our compatriots from former times who are stumbling around looking for answers, while continuing to engage in self-serving activity, and thrashing out at those who stand in their way.

So many concentrations of past energy are currently revealing their deeper secrets and making comprehensible the desires and inconsistencies flaring up, that otherwise would seem to bear no relation to the present reality. Only then can they be resolved.

Across the world, complex bits of the past are being worked on. The big issues, often poorly integrated configurations, are preventing the intended global harmony unfolding, for individual karma inevitably leads into local misjudgements, community karma reinforces the national variety, and national selfishness underpins global disarray. Every citizen of this Earth must deal with these at their source, for each one of us is part of that source. The antidotes residing in the ethers of our Earth, that were placed there by the great souls of yesteryear, are now available to any sincere group or individual with the will to access them.

## The Soul Invasion

Just how well humanity negotiates the time ahead is certainly dependent on how we choose to treat the Earth. Global warming is on everyone's lips, but science will solve many of the issues soon. It is the population explosion that is causing so much of the degradation of the planet and this will be the greatest threat to global sustainability in the coming times. So, why are there so many souls on the planet at present? It is clear that Earth cannot only be peopled by those who have been here before. Where do the rest come from?

I would estimate that over fifty percent of the current population of Earth are having their first incarnation in a physical body. They were roused from their seed source before they were prepared for life on the physical plane. They have been pulled into incarnation against their will, far ahead of their time.

Global greed is a force that sucks at all those too weak or immature to resist. The ones who wish power for themselves are always ready to commandeer more of it from wherever they can. In every country, what has been taken by these power mongers leaves a vacuum that needs to be replenished. New, young souls can provide further energy fodder for these 'vampires'.

The ones being used in this way can easily be persuaded to hate other groups who wish to share the scarce resources. They become 'the enemy who will take everything', so they are brutally attacked. Large families are encouraged, with even more of their kind dragged from the plane of pre-physical existence. You saw this with the Hutus and the Tutsis in Africa. The leaders of both sides were spurred on by various factions of the shadow band to carry out the atrocities. And you see it with some of the leaders of the mightier nations who wish to destroy independent initiative and self reliance globally by using the acquisitive corporate machine to sequester more power and privilege for themselves.

These young souls were due to have a life on the planet in, well over a thousand years time when the Aquarian energy has subsided from its peak. They aren't benefiting from being in a world that is spiritually far beyond their capabilities, and instead of experiencing the Aquarian build up from the plane of preparation, where there is far less pressure on them, they are imbibing the intoxicating energies of human existence without being able to handle their effects.

When passing on to the astral plane, they feel lost and abandoned and, rather like children wanting full adult privileges, they look to the Earth for the heady sense of invincibility they crave, for they remember their vicious leaders and want to emulate them. Of course, another life will overload them still further, causing an even greater set-back in their overall evolutionary progression.

A child dies of starvation and, soon after, a new incarnation from the same source has begun in the same sex body, in the same village, maybe even in the same family, without first integrating what they have experienced previously. They know the people, they feel at home, but they still cannot work with the energies found there.

The source selves of such people normally need very long periods of assimilation before they could usefully send a further soul to attempt even a basic Earth experience, but here they are, incarnating over and over, mainly in third world countries, without the Lords of Karma getting a look in.

It is like an addiction from which they learn little and understand less. It is all beyond their capabilities, but they want to be 'in on the act' as the Aquarian waves of upliftment come in. Alas, they are building up a store of retrogressive experience that is shared by all their former lives caught on the very lowest levels of the astral plane, and this is placing a serious restriction on their source self that will be difficult to free up when it is actually time for another life on Earth.

**The Centre Point of Evolution**
There is a span of evolution expressed by the assortment of individual souls projected from your higher self, and this is balanced at the mid point of the range. In order to lift the whole up a notch, it is particularly important that the unresolved issues of those least spiritually mature are concentrated on now.

Likewise, the propulsion that can carry humanity forward is found at the central evolutionary position of the global population and, because of the massive number of young souls incarnate today, this is in a very lowered state. We have the whole weight of their immaturity on our shoulders, and we are struggling to rise above it.

Every effort is being taken on the inner planes to convince these premature ones to hold back, but they continue to incarnate with no real understanding of what they are doing. Of course, once they are here, we must not reject them or deny them their basic needs but, at the same time, in our meditations, we can encourage them to stop their senseless determination to be incarnate. The major religions, who expect a high birth rate from their followers, must be urged to modify their teachings, and governments need to introduce incentives to keep the population low. All of this may seem hard, but the future of the planet depends on it.

You might ask why those on the inner planes who advocate a much reduced global population are not instigating plagues to remove them, but natural law determines that nothing can be done by the higher ones except when we play our equal part. It is a shared responsibility. The planetary guardians can only match our actions but, eventually, the intensity of the developing Aquarian energy will become intolerable for most of these premature souls, and the world's population will decrease quite dramatically to a more manageable level. Nevertheless, while they are here, they are providing the western world with many humanitarian lessons.

Of course, not all people in the developing nations are premature. Many started their first incarnation cycle at the time of the later Pharoahs of Ancient Egypt, very often as slaves.

And there is another category of souls I must mention which had one or more full cycles of incarnation and then went off to explore other realms and experiences away from the Earth. They have returned at this time to take advantage of the heightened energies but, in the interim, they have lost some sense of what it means to be human. They can draw on certain instinctual skills, particularly in music and dance, and are far ahead of the souls having their very first lives on a physical planet. Even so, they have a fairly immature attitude to life, and they are particularly unsuited to urban situations.

They are found in very tight knit communities in some of the Moslem countries, unable to see beyond the rigid fundamentalist beliefs. Being relatively inexperienced in the ways of the world, they are easily caught up in the more immature movements there, the suppression of women, the terrorist initiatives, for they are easily manipulated by the older, but certainly not wiser members of their extended soul families. Their retrogressive behaviour is saddling them with a great deal of negativity that will hamper their progress in lives to come.

Of course, such immaturity is not only found in the developing world, you see it in revivalist religious settings in small-town America. There is a particularly regrettable situation in Australia involving the indigenous people who live in squalid circumstances, with easy access to the alcohol they cannot handle. There is child abuse and a great deal of violence. They are not properly listened to by the liberal white authorities who expect them to conform to the same patterns of assimilation experienced by their mixed race compatriots. Unlike in most parts of Africa, this is a more manageable situation; if handled well, it could be a model for how things could progress elsewhere.

There have been so many instances where the more advanced members of the human family have tried to inflict order and their 'civilised' values onto the developing world by force, and then expected them to govern themselves without the spiritual maturity to do so. Most of the current aid programmes only breed more corruption and little self reliance. Our priorities have been terribly skewed in all sorts of awful ways brought over from the past, and we aren't learning fast enough.

We would all like to see an ordered world, run by mature people, not the usual impostors, where special enclaves of young souls can be concentrated, and that will require laws and procedures that are appropriate to their specific needs. In a way, they are still children. In earlier times, these souls would have incarnated in isolated villages and developed themselves very simply. But today, these elementary learning environments have been invaded by 'advanced' civilisation.

Always, those who are experienced in the ways of brutality are trying to seize power over their young charges. Do we, in the West, impose our will to rectify the situation or do we turn a blind eye? If we intervene and get caught up in the intractability of it all, the contentious forces found there can easily corrupt our own. It's a matter of timing, really, and motive. Alas, so many of our governments are riddled with factions and self interest, a collection of relatively evolved souls who have not yet learnt to keep their egos in check.

## Unblocking the Piscean Karma

The Earth supports a wide mix of evolution extending down from the most elevated souls in our midst, with a long history of lives since Lemurian times, who are working to remove the most severe concentrations of karma in the Earth atmosphere that they helped to establish. It is hard to believe that our world leaders are some of the most mature souls in the groups they represent. They have been incarnating for many thousands of years and don't seem to have learnt much. However, in many cases, they are considerably more advanced overall than their present behaviour would suggest. They are expressing the lower levels of their incarnational range and so, are exhibiting the most incomplete and unbalanced aspects of their source whole.

Many of us have come back expecting that the influx of high Aquarian energy will lift us out of some of our earthbound states of mind, to clear the way for an incarnation of pure service due in the 22nd century. We created much of the karma that continues to engulf the world and so, we are the obvious ones to clear it. Although we come from one of the pioneer bands of souls nearing the end of a very long incarnation cycle, most of us still have a sizeable backlog of karma to work through before we will be able to demonstrate our full maturity.

As we advance into the Aquarian age, it is vital that this global backlog is removed and the new energies can enter unimpeded. We all need to unload as much baggage as possible to free up our own evolutionary flow, so that the next life sent out from our source will be able to make use of these new energies more easily than is possible at present.

It would be unpleasant if the next life finds itself grappling with the same old misaligned and misguided energies when many others in its spirit family are free of this and are enjoying a lighter load. The new Aquarian energies can really make a difference, so it is self interest along with an underlying altruistic motive that has caused many of us to return at this time.

**Advanced Souls**
There is a final, much smaller, group of advanced souls, who had previously incarnated on other planets, walking among us now to help planet Earth successfully negotiate this major transition time. Some of these are called 'indigo children'. Most are not standing out, in fact, many are autistic, because their first wave is still having great difficulty handling the different energies to be found here. In cases where their special abilities are recognised, overzealous parents and others are promoting them as special. They need to ignore these attempts to push them forward too early. Their gifts must be stabilised so that the next generation of these souls coming in now will be able to fit in much better than they can, enabling them to play substantial roles behind the scenes of world affairs.

I think that goes some way to explain the billions of additional souls currently on the planet. It is likely that, by the end of this century, the population of the Earth will return to well under half the present level, as the various premature spirits adjust to their true position in the scheme of things and are ready to wait for a more appropriate time for another foray into Earth existence.

# 14

# Future Plans

With such a large cumbersome body, the planet evolves much more slowly than we do; it works to a different rhythm. So, when the more advanced members of the human family have achieved a high degree of mastery over what Earth could ask of them, perhaps around twelve hundred years time, the top scientists, the great composers, the visionaries, will move on to other places in the Universe to continue their evolution. Soul groups which started a little later in the Lemurian times will replace them in the vanguard of the next phase of human development. This means that some of the scientific advances that have been introduced recently, and most of what will follow, will then be out of their reach.

At that time, the influx of many young souls will lower the overall tone of humanity still further. It won't be until the last decades of this age that there will be another surge of scientific discovery, though probably not much beyond what we have achieved up to this point. As in the sea, some waves rise higher than others, and our time is especially uplifted.

The universe evolves and we are here to experience what lies between expansion and contraction, between spiralling in and spiralling out, and the enlightenment that exists when we surrender to the great Zen revelation, that we are both everything and nothing simultaneously, both dark and light in perfect balance. However, the human mind has a lot of evolving to do before it can reach a full appreciation of these matters.

**Future Lives**
As there is no time in true reality where everything is precisely aligned, there must surely be future lives in existence to balance the past ones. You may have seen those fascinating time-travel stories

## Future Plans

where people go back to change the past so that the awful future that is foreseen will not then happen, but of course, it doesn't work that way. Only the present can be transformed.

The integrated source self knows entirely which aspects of itself need further development. The Lords of Karma are already supporting group initiatives in a number of countries where karma was previously incurred and you are moving towards a rendezvous with one of them. But, until that time is reached, plans can be altered as new experiences and understanding stream into the source self from you and all your former lives. The seed self, next in line, is already dreaming of what it might become.

Let's take an actual sequence of future incarnations that I know are being considered for a man who incarnated in this life to serve the sick, the lonely, and the dispossessed. Along the way, it was expected he would develop as a healer, and he did. Earlier, he had studied law at university, but did not go on with it as a career. Nevertheless, he retained a fascination with legal matters and at various times he was threatened by an officious bureaucracy for minor transgressions. He really enjoyed outwitting the authorities in court and he regularly skirted around the law for his own ends.

Now, if we look back in time, we see that he was a particularly unscrupulous judge in a former life in Copenhagen, quite capable of twisting the law to suit his malicious nature and ingrained prejudices. He often threw people into jail without good reason, a pawn in the power system of that time. There was little understanding of true justice

It would also be seen that later on in another incarnation as a slave owner in Louisiana during the early days of that colony, he inflicted a severe regime on his charges. Eventually they rose up and slaughtered him. The so-called justice meted out on those slaves was even more harsh than it had been when he was a judge. He had learned nothing.

He also cruelly dominated his family, particularly the female members, and he barely shed a tear when his wife died of consumption. All the love and support he could muster was for his son who went on to become even more ruthless with the slaves than he had been.

At this present time, the next seed self is beginning to make sense of these components, and is tentatively preparing for a career in law. Will it be as a judge? That is unlikely, because the judge of old has not made sufficient progress in his understanding of justice, in the interim, for this to be productive. The Lords of Karma are well aware of the full picture and are not going to recommend a role where he will over-reach himself. No, it will be as a judge's clerk, observing how justice works from the sidelines which will give him the necessary compassion to effectively support a life as a judge later on.

Most significantly, this incarnation will be experienced in a mixed race body in Atlanta, Georgia where many of his spirit family will be incarnating. The wife, in the Louisiana incarnation is likely to be his wife in this new Southern environment. This life is still perhaps twenty five years away and, as time passes, the details will become more precise. Some components may be changed, but the three most important lessons, understanding justice, valuing people of all races and cultures, and respecting women, will probably not alter because these spiritual qualities will be vital to the life following on from that one.

I have stressed that three major past lives are usually incorporated into any destiny plan, so a third needs to be added to the ones from Copenhagen and Louisiana. There are several possibilities. In a Swiss life, he had been extremely incensed at the treatment of the farm workers and labourers who were dependent on powerful land owners and businessmen for their livelihood. They were forced to live in appalling conditions on a paltry wage.

As a member of a once well-off family that had suffered under the quiet tyranny of this system, he was strongly motivated to reveal the ways of these landowners and their network of control. He had a fiery, passionate temperament, and was determined to stand up to these men, to expose their 'wickedness'. He tried to get the workers to join him, but they were too cowed to respond. Even his wife would not support him, so he ventured out on a one-man crusade to right these wrongs. Unfortunately, he did not exercise enough caution and he quickly became a thorn in the side of the authorities. This reckless attempt to bring justice to the oppressed was totally misguided, and he was assassinated at the age of 28.

There is another possible life, but it is not certain it would be wise to include any more extremely callous energies in the background. As a wealthy land-owner in China, brother to a mandarin of the Ming dynasty, he had treated people very brutally. Indeed, when he caught a neighbour's son stealing apples from his tree, he beat him soundly and the lad suffered crippling injuries. He could not know that, in later lives, this young thief would develop an equally violent nature and would be responsible for many deaths. So, now this lad has to experience a life in a deformed body needing constant care, and this will most likely be as the son of the law clerk.

Already, there is quite enough material to build up a substantial destiny pattern but when the time comes for that life to be prepared, additional past influences may be chosen, and others discarded. Free will always takes precedence over such planning, and the Lords of Karma have other options in mind should a shift in direction become necessary.

**The Life Following That**
In his early days of this present life, our protagonist showed no interest in politics. He did not join a political party, believing that they were all self-serving phonies and, for a long time, he didn't vote when election time came around. Nevertheless he wrote and acted in a number of plays with strong political themes, attended demonstrations against the Vietnam War, and imagined himself as a leader with superior ideas on how to run the country.

All this experience will be important for the lifetime that will follow the legal one. It will be in the coming century when the Aquarian consciousness is fully active in the world. The extended spirit family has already decided to focus all its human resources into one particularly important mission. For most of them, it will be a major life arising out of a minor preparatory one which is, of course, what the courtroom life in Atlanta will be.

And where will this happen? In Corsica, and the extended spirit family will effectively run that country. By then, there will be a good balance of men and women in authority positions.

This person will wish to be given an influential role in the political arena. It will depend on the aggregate of evolution achieved by the source self as to how much responsibility can be taken on. Don't forget, it is the less accomplished members of the spirit family that are having their concerns met through lives on Earth today. So, there will be far more evolved past personalities available to support this political incarnation. One had been a senior student of Socrates in ancient Greece who had often taught lessons for that great man, while not, it must be admitted, fully understanding them at the time. This is the most mature projection from the oversoul and he is likely to be the main inspiration for this important Corsican life.

The law clerk will be the fourth male incarnation in a row, so it is necessary to experience this life in a female body. Male lives, however sympathetic they may be towards women, however much the yin aspect is cultivated, are no substitute for the real thing; and it will be a thirteenth life.

It is necessary to look to previous leadership incarnations for the second of the three major backing lives. All of them have progressed since they left the Earth, and some of the more reprehensible characters have gone on to become quite saintly with the passage of time. There is a hidebound army general from Ancient Egypt at the time of Akhenaten who had opposed the work of that great visionary; and a life which was quite high up in the army of the Holy Roman Empire. More recently there was a warlord in Afghanistan. Not a set of lives to bring a humane attitude to conflict into the present, you might think, but these three have learnt a great deal subsequently on how to handle aggression. However, only one of them can be chosen to give lifetime backing to this important political mission.

The Roman general had developed considerable courage during that life, and behaved very reasonably towards any of the enemy who were captured. He had begun to look more deeply within himself and this introspection was further developed when he backed a later life as a holy man in an ashram in southern India dedicated to non-violence. This Roman influence will serve the politician very well in her attempts to bring the very conservative Corsica into more inclusive, non-judgemental ways of social interaction.

The third over-arching life will need to have been lived in a female body to bring a compassionate element into the psyche. One possibility incarnated as a member of the Parisian aristocracy and fled to London just prior to the French Revolution. Her husband stayed behind and had his head lopped off on the guillotine.

The few jewels she took with her provided insufficient funds to continue her extravagant lifestyle, but some friends amongst the English nobility helped out. In the period before her death in a street accident, she became very involved with a philanthropist and his wife who ministered tirelessly to the poor. This charitable work will stand her in good stead in addressing social inequality in her life as a politician.

She will retain a very ambivalent attitude towards France, for Corsica is a French protectorate, and there will be a great deal of meddling in Corsican affairs by that country. This will lead to a cessation movement that will engage her sympathies.

The second possible female influence incarnated as the wife of an important adviser in the court of Frederick Barbarossa, a twelfth century Spanish ruler. In playing the role of dutiful spouse, she paid a great deal of attention to the detail of the social calendar. She also developed a skill in gaining favours, and considerable aptitude in running the large mansion while caring for the many servants and farm workers on her estate. She learned how to get the best out of them without resorting to the kind of authoritarian approach favoured by her husband. In other words, she became wise in the ways of diplomacy and peaceful human inter-relation, not insignificant attributes for a politician to have.

As I have said, this is all pure conjecture at this time, though clearly, the process is not begun when people die, and they look down at Earth and think, "I wonder what I should do next." It is much more intricately planned ahead of time than that.

However, the lead up to lives does not always work out as expected and the eventual composition of this Corsican incarnation is completely dependent on free will operating over the ninety or so years ahead and on the opportunities that are there to be taken when the time comes. Nevertheless, preparation for it will continue on all levels, with adjustments regularly being made.

So, that Corsican experience may need to start and develop somewhere else, in Paris perhaps, where she could start her political career and only later become the French ambassador to Corsica. There are usually a number of ways to reach a particular destination and, in this case, the exact path is far from fixed. The Lords of Karma are consistently shaping the needs of the oversoul into possible future formations, and the relevant seeds within the source are gradually awakening to what may lie ahead. They feel that it will be a very beautiful thing to be both human and divinely connected, but they don't realise the extent that this link will be obscured once they incarnate.

A political life in a female body will require great resilience and the ability to stand up to the regressive actions and hidden motives of the more avid power mongers who will certainly be there to challenge her. Not all men in the family of souls will have given up trying to gain power for themselves. So, in order to forge a path of truth and justice in political life, the ability to stand firm, as Gandhi did, will have to be honed over the century still to come. There will be plenty of opportunities to develop the qualities needed.

Few people realise the extent to which evil is the servant of good. But when they have progressed along the path, have faced the shadow elements in themselves, and have learned to lift the weaknesses as well as the more refined qualities to the Father, they will begin to know, without doubt, that they are taking part in the work of liberating mother Earth while, in the process, liberating themselves.

## Finally

Well, that almost completes my presentation of this vast subject. There are many more components of it and a number of quite different incarnation patterns that some people experience. I have explored the usual ways that Serial Consciousness works on our planet. However, it is really only a half the picture, because duality in the Godhead actually spawns much more complex patterns of incarnation than I have outlined, when the source self is more mature.

I hope to have laid to rest some common misconceptions. I have called this book Serial Consciousness while recognising that the term reincarnation is so ingrained that this expression may not take off but, nevertheless, it is much more accurate. The source self cannot incarnate in its entirety. The parts of itself, sent out as apparently separate expressions of consciousness, remain at large in the same inner space after the life is over. This has probably been your soul's only incarnation in human form. It is precious.

Even if you do complete your destiny agenda, it is unlikely to be the end of the line. There are probably other former lives who have not attained your level of elevation and who will need their concerns addressed through a future life. We would all like to be permanently off the wheel of Earth karma, but for most of us, this is an unrealistic and, indeed, rather selfish ideal.

You will continue to grow in stature and influence, no matter where you choose to be in the creation, but your roots will remain in the Earth which is still far from its apotheosis. You will continue as an individual, in some form, indefinitely and this, I am sure, is the way you would wish it to be.

**Advanced Souls**

When Jesus came to Earth, his source self had already experienced human life in many bodies, including one as Zoroaster. There is no longer any need for further physical experience. Jesus continues to exist on a high level of the third plane serving humanity from there. However, there are many source entities that have sent down souls that achieved a measure of greatness in their time and are continuing to project consciousness into human form, each with a mission to assist humanity in its struggle to release the remaining karma still very active on the planet today.

Rudolph Steiner stays close to the organisation he founded, though he is far from happy with the way it is progressing. He wishes that they would listen to what he is saying now rather than following what he taught when on Earth. Alongside this, a further expression of that same oversoul is incarnate, in female form this time, and she is delving deeply into the creative power of the earth by working directly with Gaia, and the nature spirits. She is preparing for the male life to follow that will confirm the mastery that eluded Steiner.

The source that gave life to the master Socrates has sent down a number of subsequent incarnations, most significantly in South America. What was set into place energetically during that very important Earth mission is now beginning to bear fruit. There is a life projection from the same oversoul currently in South Africa working quietly to counter the shadow forces that are trying to take control there. His is truly an energy of the light.

In the coming centuries, lives will tend to be longer than they are at present. Earth existence is such a fleeting thing, a small part of you in your entirety. Although you are but one of an extensive cycle of lives, you are the only one who can presently release the secrets of human evolution. In that sense, you are all powerful. When faced with the apparent insignificance of your life, I would recommend that you do not see yourself as just a small fraction of the whole, you are a half. There is you and there is everything else, two equal parts of the whole. This will enable you to feel yourself to be an entirely effective player in your life, a true creator, not insignificant at all. It is the ego that judges your worth, always to your detriment.

You are perfect as you are, perfectly who you are. Without you, this vast creation would not exist. One small part missing in an aircraft and it cannot fly. The large and the small are totally dependent on each other and it is by accepting your immense worth that your universal nature comes into prominence. Inadequacy is not a concept that the masters recognise. Guilt does not exist in their vocabulary, or shame. Let go of such concepts, and your mind will be filled with unconditonal light and divine dark in perfect harmony.

The dark and the shadow are not the same. The former speaks of the glory of the human experience rooted deep and standing tall, like a giant redwood in the forest of life. By drawing up nourishment from the dense fertile soil and drawing in the rays of the celestial Sun, you exist magnificently.

A visionary sees only what is truly there. An avatar no longer values separation. "Love thy neighbour as thyself," says it all. In the field of Serial Consciousness, everything leads into everything else. It is not really about returning home to the place that you have never left, to the Divine source that is you. It is about embracing your current test, your present opportunity for initiation, with immense joy in your heart.

Know that your journey is a perfect progression, and that your family of souls is forever seeking to be re-united in every moment without cause and effect marring that perfection. Be at one with yourself, at one with all others, and totally free. Be simply what is, no more and no less, for that is all any of us will ever be.

**Other titles from 'Eye of Gaza Press':**

# New Dimensions in Healing
## Tony Neate

The new millennium requires widened concepts and subtler, deeper ways of healing. This book breaks fresh ground, exploring advanced specialist healing modalities. It recommends the rigorous development of both the psychic and spiritual selves. It gives clear advice on many ways of reaching the cause of the illness.

Tony Neate has been a respected spiritual teacher since the mid 1950's and a practitioner particularly in the field of life threatening illness. He was chair of the Holistic Council for cancer, and he co-founded both the College of Healing and the Confederation of Healing Organisations.

IBSN 1 873545 04 5          148 pp

# Secrets of Planet Earth
## Tony Neate

This challenging work lifts the lid on society and the natural order to expose the hidden forces behind science, religion, politics and international unrest. His remit stretches far back in time to include Atlantis, and forward to an uncertain future. It provides startling revelations for our times and is a vital read for all our leaders, indeed, anyone concerned about the future of the planet. At the heart of this book is great wisdom and boundless compassion.

*"These are ideas which I personally had not come across before and are well worth pondering. His words have the ring of authority and of truth."*
Light Magazine.

# The Spirit Within
## Ivy Northage

For over 50 years Ivy Northage has been a widely respected and much loved deep trance medium and her spirit guide, Chan, has an understanding of the purpose of life that is far beyond our limited human vision. His approach is always practical, sensible and fully comprehensive, and he unfolds it with an uncompromising intellectual rigour that encourages us to take a deep focused look at our attitudes and motives.

IBSN 1 873545 03 7         148 pp

## Some useful contacts:

Helios School of Healing,
116 Judd Street,
London, WC1H 9NS

Phone: 0207 713 7120
heliosc@dialstart.net
www.helioshealth.org.uk

Tony Neate
10 Hatley Court
81 Albert Road South,
Worcs, WR14 3DX

Phone: 01684 893697
tony-neate@tiscali.co.uk
www.channelling-online.com

Greg Branson
45c St Augustine's Road,
London, NW1 9RL

Phone: 0207 713 7159
heliosc@dialstart.net
www.heliosenlighten.org

Spirit Release Foundation
Frida Siton
Myrtles, Como Road,
Malvern, WR14 3TH

Phone: 01684 560725
fridamaria@spiritrelease.com
www.spiritrelease.com